CALIFORNIA STATE UNIVERSITY, SACRAMENTO

This book is due on the last da†
Failure to return books on the dc
sessment of overdue fees.

CSUS LIBRARY

JUN 1 0

The Collected Poems of

Thomas and Jane Welsh Carlyle

Impressions of Thomas and Jane Welsh Carlyle, circa 1822
by Robert D. Sutherland
July, 1981

The Collected Poems of

Thomas and Jane Welsh Carlyle

Edited by

Rodger L. Tarr

and

Fleming McClelland

ৠ

with a foreword by
G. B. Tennyson

.

The Penkevill Publishing Company
Greenwood Florida

Copyright © 1986
Rodger L. Tarr and Fleming McClelland

ISBN 0-913283-09-6

Printed in the United States of America

For

Carol Anita

and

Mary Anne

Preface

The intent of this volume is not to spring upon the unsuspecting the poetic profundities of two potential laureates. Written for the most part in that state of volatile flux when Britain was plodding toward Victorian reform, these poems are strangely removed, quiescent, outside the vulgarity of commonness. Romantic in spirit, pre-Reform in attitude, they ring with the sense of juvenalia, measured and unmeasured in their curious blend of the foreboding and the lovely. They represent the collision of Calvinist values during the eighteen-twenties, what might be called the Scottish paradox. East meets West here — East and West in Scotland, that is. These are the poems of a socialite's daughter from fashionable Haddington and of a peasant's son from provincial Ecclefechan. They are the compositions of innocents who were struggling to survive the Byronic distemper that had become a part of the post-Regency psyche. The poets are Thomas and Jane Welsh Carlyle of Scotland, the soon to become legends of London literati.

To be certain, no claim can be made for the Carlyles as poets extraordinaire. Yet there are those haunting moments when Burns, Byron, even Wordsworth swim into ken. And, of course, Goethe and the Germanic tradition of transcendence loom large upon the horizon. In fact, it is the unusual confluence of mainland with continent that lends an intriguing eclecticism to the Carlyles' poetry. They write in many forms, in many traditions; and they seem painfully aware that theirs were talents without limitless potential. They were, as Professor Tennyson suggests in his Foreword, frustrated poets, interlopers into a genre that was not altogether comfortable to them. Still, both were as poetic as possible without being poetic — at least in the practising sense — at all. In the case of Carlyle, who rejected poetry for prose after a fleeting moment with fiction, the immediate loss was ultimately the world's gain. He became the master of a prose style precisely because he was innately poetic. His enduring prose models, like *Sartor Resartus* and *The French Revolution,* are appealing exactly because of their kinship to poetry, what Emerson was later to describe as Carlyle's Homeric instinct. As for Jane Welsh, her poems represent, except for brief fictional forays, most of what we know about her latent literary talent. Thus, when we judge the Carlyles as poets, we should do so in context. Their poems are not the products of self-proclaimed advocates; quite the opposite, they are the private, sometimes very personal, issue of two of Victoria's most celebrated subjects.

The purpose, then, of this edition is to bring together the published and unpublished poetry of the Carlyles, exclusive of the occasional unidentified — and perhaps unidentifiable — couplets that are scattered here and there in Carlyle's writings. Insofar as the translations are concerned, only those which seem to have been intended as individual poems are included, and no attempt has been made to reproduce the hundreds of poetic fragments that can be found throughout the works on German literature. Finally, a few ballads that Carlyle adapted and treated as his own are included, as are some verses that he often used as autograph samples and some poems of questionable attribution.

As always a great many debts are owed in a project of this kind, and the editors wish to express special gratitude to the following: To K. J. Fielding, Ian Campbell, and John Hall of the University of Edinburgh for supplying texts and confirming readings; to Clyde de L. Ryals of Duke University for his reading of and contribution to the manuscript; to Alan Bell, Librarian Rhodes House Library, Oxford; to Thomas I. Rae, I. F. Mciver, and Elspeth Yeo of the National Library of Scotland, for seeing to the location and reproduction of manuscripts; to the authorities of the Houghton Reading Room, Harvard University; the New York Public Library, Berg Collection; and the Henry E. Huntington Library; to R. L. Davids of Sotheby's, London; and especially to Marjorie Wynne of the Beinecke Library, Yale University — to all our sincere and warm thanks.

Other individuals whom we wish to thank for their help and courtesies are Richard Tobias of the University of Pittsburgh; George O. Marshall, Jr., William R. Thurman, Ben Teague, and Susanna Wagner of the University of Georgia; Suzanne Rutter, Christa Sammons, and

Stephen R. Parks at Yale; Dr. Gerhard Schmid of the Goethe-Schiller Archiv, Weimar; Colonel James Edgar, Curator of the Carlyle House in Chelsea; Pamela White and Margaret M. Smith of the *Index of English Literary Manuscripts,* London; Mr. and Mrs. George Armour; Miss Lillias B. Brown; Mrs. Mary Harland; Mrs. Elizabeth J. Mitchell; and Mr. David O. C. Mitchell.

Last but not least, our special thanks to Professor G. B. Tennyson of the University of California, Los Angeles, for writing in his usual inimitable style the Foreword; and to Robert D. Sutherland, colleague, for his original ink impressions of the Carlyles in 1822.

We gratefully acknowledge the following institutions for granting permission to print Carlyle manuscript materials from their holdings: Beinecke Library, Yale University; National Library of Scotland; the National Trust, London; Victoria and Albert Museum; Harvard University Library; the Henry E. Huntington Library; the Goethe-Schiller Archiv, Weimar; and the Berg Collection, New York Public Library.

R. L. T.
F. M.

To Illinois State University for grants in support, my acknowledgement; and to the Fulbright Commission, for naming me a Senior Research Scholar in Great Britain, my particular acknowledgement.

Rodger L. Tarr

CONTENTS

Impressions of the Carlyles in 1822
by Robert D. Sutherland

ILLUSTRATIONS

Foreword

In the scholarship and criticism on Thomas Carlyle few words appear more frequently than the words relating to poetry — *poet, poetic, poetical, epic poem,* and of course the word *poetry* itself. Yet Carlyle is the author of only a few hundred lines of original verse, and that verse is almost totally unknown. But the terms relating to poetry are, of course, applied to Carlyle's *prose.* A representative statement comes from Emerson as early as 1853, who, after speaking of Carlyle's humor, writes:

> The other particular of magnificence is in his rhymes. Carlyle is a poet who is altogether too burly in his frame and habit to submit to the limits of metre. Yet he is full of rhythm not only in the perpetual melody of his periods, but in the burdens, refrains, and grand returns of his sense and music.

Emerson would probably not have been moved to speak so favorably of Carlyle's actual rhymes, had he known them. But Emerson does put his finger on qualities that are genuinely there in Carlyle's prose. It is well to ponder for a moment just what those qualities are in Carlyle's prose the better to understand their absence in his poetry.

First, however, we must understand something of the all-purpose character of the words *poet* and *poetry* in nineteenth-century literary discourse. When commentators like Emerson speak of Carlyle's prose as poetry they are speaking a language that derives from the Romantics early in the century for whom poetry was not only the ultimate literary form but also an activity that defined the artist. It means a making more than an imitating, and it involves inspiration and prophecy as much as writing in metre. Wordsworth even went so far as to say that "poetry is the breath and finer spirit of all knowledge, it is the impassioned expression which is in the countenance of all Science."

For the rest of the century such sentiments were echoed and expanded, so that the poetry family of terms did more than take up the slack caused by the nineteenth-century obsolescence of the old inclusive term *poesy*. Eventually poetry-terms came to serve in English almost as *Dichter* and *dichten* do in German, where *Dichter* can mean both a poet and a writer in general and *dichten* can mean to compose a literary work whether in verse or prose. Typically Carlyle himself carried the use of poetry-terms to their nineteenth-century extreme when he wrote in his *Cromwell*: "He that works and *does* some Poem not he that merely *says* one, is worthy of the name of Poet." Carlyle has come perilously close to divesting poetry and related terms even of literary associations. But for the most part the terms stayed in the realm of art, if not narrowly of literature, and we still today encounter expressions like "the poetry of architecture" that testify to the endurance of the distinctive nineteenth-century use of poetry-terms outside the domain of verse alone.

When poetry-terms were applied to Carlyle's prose, as in the instance cited from Emerson, they were meant to convey, first, a favorable judgment, to convince the reader that the author in question was an artist and not a mere conveyor of fact, or as the Victorians would have said, not a conveyor of mere fact. Second, they were meant to give the reader a sense of just what special kind of artistry the author was engaged in. It was that sort of writing that was heightened and intensified above ordinary speech or writing, the sort the Victorians would have held was noble. More than that, it was the use of words in such a way as to convey what Owen Barfield in our time came to call a "felt change of consciousness" on the part of the reader as he perceived these particular words in this particular order. We can remember here Coleridge's definition of poetry as the best words in the best order. That critics felt that a poetic effect could be brought about in what is technically prose as well as in what is technically poetry meant that they would surely find that effect in the prose of Thomas Carlyle. Thus George Eliot said that Carlyle was "more of an artist than a philosopher," that he was one of those writers who "strikes you, undeceives you, animates you . . . you are braced as by a walk up to an alpine summit, and yet subdued to calm and reverence as by the sublime things to be seen from that summit." One can think of countless passages from Carlyle's prose that would lead readers to such a judgment. If that is what poetry means, Carlyle in prose is indeed a poet.

When we turn to the verse of this master of poetic prose, however, the question that inevitably arises is why, by comparison with the prose, is Carlyle's poetry so, well, unpoetic? Emerson opined that Carlyle's poetry in prose was a sort that did not let itself be readily confined. That certainly is part of the answer. The nature of Carlyle's prose-poetry is expansive, outward moving, soaring, large in spirit and vision. He gains many of his effects by the sheer magnitude of his utterance. All this has to do with Carlyle's view of what is fit to be called poetry, the view that he inherited from the Romantics and himself carried even further than they. Throughout the eighteen-twenties Carlyle was forging a literary vision that amalgamated prophecy, religion, social commentary, and history, and that did so under the generous rubric of poetry. Such a conception hardly lends itself to the technical constraints of stanza and metre.

Yet when we come to Carlyle's verse as such it is precisely the presence of stanza and metre that we encounter. His verse falls into limited and prescribed stanzaic patterns, often those of ballad metre or common metre, the kind of poetry that Carlyle would have known from his earliest childhood. See, for example, the intriguing Carlyle hymn, "Wandering in a Strange Land." Carlyle's efforts in verse seem directed toward the pithy and the compact. There is little of that large outward moving thrust of his prose. If I may be permitted some speculation, I would say that Carlyle's attitude toward verse (as opposed to his attitude toward that larger area that he was willing to call poetry) may have to do with a Puritan distrust of verse as such, which could only be overcome by equating poetry with any form of lofty writing, including prose. Prose is, after all, the instrument of the preacher; poetry by contrast may be the instrument of the dilettante. Moreover, Carlyle himself was fond of referring to poetry narrowly construed as "song." To Carlyle song meant border ballads, the "airs" of lowland Scotland that in later years Jane used to delight him with by her piano playing in their Chelsea home. In his essay on

Burns Carlyle reserved his highest praise for Burns's "Songs":

> Independently of the clear, manly, heartfelt sentiment that
> ever pervades his poetry, his Songs are honest in another
> point of view; in form, as well as in spirit. They do not
> *affect* to be set to music, but they actually and in them-
> selves are music, they have received their life, and fashioned
> themselves together, in the medium of Harmony, as Venus
> rose from the bosom of the sea. The story, the feeling,
> is not detailed, but suggested; not *said,* or spouted, in rhe-
> torical completeness and coherence; but *sung,* in fitful
> gushes, in glowing hints, in fantastic breaks, in warblings not
> of the voice only, but of the whole mind.

It is the effect of Burns's songs, I believe, that Carlyle strove for in
his own verse. At times indeed he almost attains some of this, as in
the songlike "Lasses of the Cannongate" (is it indeed original with
Carlyle, one wonders) and in some of the other verse with Scottish
sounds and associations, including especially some of his light and
humourous "songs" on literary figures from himself to Francis Jeffrey.
But at other times Carlyle seems to be trying to achieve the songlike
effect by formula, as in "Let Time and Chance Combine, Combine."
    Thus Carlyle was restrained by a concept of poetry that was oddly
bifurcated, that was both too expansive and too narrow. On the
one hand, poetry was in his view, as in that of his Romantic pre-
decessors, elevated, noble, prophetic, visionary, all of which he realized
in his prose when he became himself the "poet-vates" he so often
spoke of. On the other hand, poetry was to be light and airy, com-
pact and direct, simple and unaffected, such as had been realized by
his compatriot Burns. Carlyle was never able to reconcile these two
perspectives within the confines of metre.
    But whatever their shortcomings as poetry, the three-score-odd
poems and translations from Carlyle's pen now brought together for
the first time do underscore some enduring truths about Carlyle.
Among these are his insistent grounding in the everyday life he first
knew as a lowland Scots peasant, a grounding that later contributed

to keeping Carlyle, as thinker and stylist, always in contact with the everyday realities of life. We see also in these verse attempts on Carlyle's part, most of them early in his career, that fascination for the past that does not degenerate into mere nostalgia but that forms part of Carlyle's lifelong awareness that the present is the past in a state of becoming. We see, too, much of what the all-powerful German experience meant to Carlyle when we note that it is almost entirely German poems that he translates, though his command of French was excellent (and prior) and his knowledge of the classical tongues not inconsiderable. All this and more can and will be distilled out of this gathering by future readers, even if at the same time this collection shows that Carlyle was right to direct his major efforts elsewhere.

On a deeper level we can see that what Carlyle did in his early attempts at verse suggests that had he persevered, he might have done original work in poetry, perhaps something as stark and rugged as Newman's verse for the *Lyra Apostolica* or even something as stark and rugged and at the same time as poignant and moving as the poetry of Thomas Hardy later in the century. Carlyle's "To-Day," one of the few of his poems that has had any currency, almost has this Hardy-like element. If one could imagine him as well still retaining the force and directness of the metrical form, one could then go on to imagine Carlyle forging for himself in poetry the same kind of original voice that makes his prose so uniquely his own.

But it was not to be, either for Carlyle or for Jane Welsh. Jane for her part is relatively more sprightly than Carlyle as poet, but her sentiments are yet more conventional. In her poem on Bryon she does capture some of the pathos of the Byron-Ada relationship, reminding us of how alive Jane was to the contemporary literary situation. It is not hard to see from that sort of intellectual alertness why it was that in letters of the same period Jane so often expresses exasperation with *Kleinstadterei* of Haddington and why she was at least as suitable and eager for the literary life of the greater world as Thomas.

In the fifteen surviving pieces by Jane there is both the hint of a literary talent gone unrealized and the quite contrary evidence that perhaps Jane had no real vocation. For on the one hand her poetry

has some of the qualities of her engaging letters that have led many
to see her as a lost literary artist, and yet on the other hand the very
slender output itself, stemming wholly from the years when she had
no burdens as Mrs. Thomas Carlyle and might have pursued her literary
interests more zealously, suggests that Jane was not a thwarted genius.
It may be that Jane's greatest talent in literature lay in inspiring others,
as certainly the finest poem in which she had a hand is Leigh Hunt's
masterly "Rondeau," best known from its opening words, "Jenny
kissed me." And her role there was simply to *be* Jenny.

One can see in Jane's translation "From East to West" something
of what it was to be Jane and why being Jane could inspire a Leigh
Hunt; for the poem has much of the shrewd, playful acuity that Jane
exhibited to the London literary circle, and one wishes she had con-
tinued to cultivate the vein of light verse. Perhaps this aspect of her
character *was,* at least in poetry, somewhat discouraged by Carlyle.
The version of Jane's translation of Goethe's "Der Fischer" that is
printed here provides an example. This is the one she adopted after
Carlyle's corrections. These are, to be sure, more faithful to the
German, but they also tone down the lighthearted translation that
Jane originally offered. In the last line of the first stanza Jane had
originally written of the fisherman: "His heart was full of joy." Car-
lyle changed "full of joy" to "Felt little joy or care," which more
accurately reflects Goethe's "Kuhl bis ans Herz hinan," but which
makes of Jane's fisherman a more sombre fellow. Likewise, in the
fourth stanza Jane had rendered Goethe's lines "Du steigst herunter
wie du bist, / Und wurdest erst gesung!" as "Thou wouldst go with
me speedily / His cool abode to seek." But she dutifully adopted the
more portentous Carlylean phrasing, "Thou'dst haste with me where
pleasure stays / To hide from toil and woe." Perhaps Jane's poem
"I Love," with its glorification of Byronic tumult and passion in praise
of the soul that rushes forward, "proud, fiery, brooking no control,"
may be taken as the expression of Jane's romantic heart, which her
poem "Nay, this is hope" with its poignant lines:

> And this is Life: ethereal fire
>
> Striving aloft through smothering clay

may be taken as her mature recognition of what the romantic heart
must actually encounter in life.

There is a sense in which the Carlyles do with poetry as they did with fiction: they experiment when young, trying their hands at various kinds of verse as they did at various kinds of fiction. One remembers Carlyle's unfinished "Wotton Reinfred" or his and Jane's barely undertaken joint epistolary novel. But neither verse nor fiction suffices. Still, there is much to be said for false starts: they help one find his right direction, and they teach lessons on the way. Jane ultimately channels her literary energies into those vivacious and glittering letters; Carlyle ultimately channels his into that extraordinary prose that is poetry even though it is not verse. When Frederick W. Faber took holy orders Wordsworth said, "England loses a poet." In a curious way, when Carlyle moves into prose rather than into poetry, we may well say, "England gains a poet."

The versifiers that England lost in Carlyle and Jane when they moved into literary areas more suited to their talents did not attract much attention *as* versifiers even after they attained eminence on other grounds. As the editors make clear in their judicious and informative Introduction, only brief notice was taken of Carlyle's poetry (and none of Jane's) in the abundance of Victorian and modern scholarship and criticism of him until my own investigation of the matter twenty years ago. That there would ever be a full-scale scholarly edition of the poetry of the two Carlyles appeared not to be a consummation very many had devoutly wished. Even I, who did so, did not expect to see such an undertaking. But in offering us precisely that full-scale scholarly edition the present editors are simultaneously satisfying and creating an interest in a worthwhile subject, much as Carlyle himself was able to discern a submerged interest in an issue (mediaeval monasticism, norse mythology, Cromwell, Frederick) and by addressing it in his compelling manner call forth an aware and engaged constituency for his topic. So the present editors have focussed upon a topic in Carlyle scholarship whose time has come. They have assembled a body of writing interesting in itself that must needs also encourage reflections on the life, the times, the literary weight of the two Carlyles, of which my foregoing remarks have been the first humble fruits.

Beyond the feat of the gathering itself, what makes the present edition so especially valuable is the supporting material the editors have provided for our understanding of the poetry. Their identification of sources, manuscripts, printed versions, and their providing of relevant background and critical material for each poem effectively put this volume into the category of a new work by the Carlyles that must command the attention of scholars and students of the Victorian age. From the materials provided by this edition we can trace, if not Carlyle's "development" as a poet, surely some of his developing interests. From this first full gathering of Jane's poetry we can glimpse again some of the qualities that made for so many of those literary pilgrimages to Chelsea in after years. All this *is* a consummation devoutly to be wished.

G. B. Tennyson

Introduction

i
The Critical Heritage

Until recently Carlyle's poetry has not been the subject of extensive critical attention, and most of the criticism that is available tends to follow Carlyle's cue in denigrating his own works. With very few exceptions commentators cite his poetry as a curiosity, or as an example of the human imperfection to which even such an otherwise gifted writer as Carlyle was subject.

Much of the early commentary on Carlyle's poetry appears in the context of biography, with James Anthony Froude leading the way. In his four volumes of Carlyle biography, Froude printed several of Carlyle's poems and offered scattered judgments on the poetic merit of some of them, the final verdict being that they generally lacked originality and that Carlyle "had no correct metrical ear" (*First Forty Years,* I, 253). Other contemporary biographers and memorialists who mentioned Carlyle's poetry may have acknowledged a personal affinity for one or two of his poems (usually "Today" or "Adieu"), but, like Froude, most found Carlyle's performance as a whole disappointing. The following entry from William Allingham's *Diary* can speak for most of the rest of Carlyle's contemporaries:

> In his verse you can hear the sound of an original man, vigour, quaintness, imagery are there, and for a few lines, less or more, the movement may go right, but only by chance; presently it goes all awry. It is not a question of choosing or happening to be rough, or of taking liberties: the Writer, after reading many thousand lines of the best Poets, remains entirely insensible to the *structure* of verse, to the indispensable rules derived from the nature of the human mind and ear.[1]

The first systematic discussions of Carlyle's poetry appeared at
the turn of the century in Germany. Heinrich Kraeger's "Carlyles
Stellung zur Deutschen Sprache und Literatur"[2] includes commentary
on the seven poems from the "Fractions" of *Critical and Miscellaneous
Essays* as well as remarks on "Peter Nimmo," "The Sigh," "Morgarten,"
and "Crichope Linn." These discussions typically present a brief sum-
mary of a poem's narrative, followed by a catalog of the poem's artistic
shortcomings — the same ones that Carlyle's British contemporaries
also lamented, with the perhaps predictable difference that Kraeger
finds a few of the poems to be little more than pale imitations of
works by Goethe and Schiller. Arthur Mämpel's *Thomas Carlyle
als Künstler*[3] took Kraeger's work as a starting point; however, Mämpel
presents a more sympathetic and balanced view of Carlyle's efforts
in verse. While he agrees that Carlyle's poetry does not belong among
the exhibits of excellence in the genre, Mämpel notes favorably the
folk qualities of the poems, Carlyle's skillful use of refrain, and his
characteristic juxtaposing of the greater and smaller worlds. Following
a basically chronological organization, Mämpel provides variously
detailed discussions for nineteen of Carlyle's poems.

By far the most important essay discussing Carlyle's poetry, however,
is G. B. Tennyson's "Carlyle's Poetry to 1840: A Checklist and Dis-
'cussion, a New Attribution, and Six Unpublished Poems" (*VP*, 1
[1963], 161-181). In his article Tennyson gives a checklist of thirty-
five of Carlyle's poems and translations up to 1840, along with dates
for composition and first publication, places of first publication, and
places of most accessible subsequent publication. Following the
checklist Tennyson presents brief discussions of all of Carlyle's listed
poems and of three of his translations. In addition to Carlyle's the-
matic concerns, Tennyson notes some characteristic Carlylean images,
notably those of the wanderer and of contrast (great and small, and
light and dark, for instance), as they appear in the poems, and he
also calls attention to some of Carlyle's typical stylistic effects. Tenny-
son concludes his article by printing the texts of six of the previously
unpublished manuscript poems from the Carlyle materials at Yale.[4]

Although they do not offer as extensive direct comments on Car-
lyle's work in poetry as do the works previously cited, several addi-

tional books and articles contain material that is pertinent to the subject of the poetry. The Duke-Edinburgh edition of the Carlyle letters, in addition to providing a wealth of biographical information, prints a few of the poems; J. M. Sloan printed "Crichope Linn" along with a picture of the linn in *The Carlyle Country*;[5] and William H. Wylie printed "Drumwhirn Bridge" in *Thomas Carlyle* and correctly conjectured, on the basis of biographical and stylistic details, that the poem was Carlyle's.[6] Positive identification of "Drumwhirn Bridge" as Carlyle's, however, came in Frank Miller's *The Poets of Dumfriesshire,* where Miller printed the poem from a manuscript that was taken from Carlyle's dictation at Craigenputtoch.[7] Miller also printed "My Own Four Walls" from a dictated manuscript and "The Sower's Song" from the *Essays* text, and he provided passing comments on some of Carlyle's other poems. Finally, D. A. Wilson printed the poem "Adieu" in *Mr. Froude and Carlyle* and made his most persuasive argument there for its association with Margaret Gordon.[8]

Of related interest are studies dealing with Carlyle's association with Goethe. Georg Hecht, for instance, printed the texts of "Scotland Prides" and "All mute and dim as Shadows gray," as well as a facsimile of the manuscript of "For th' Heaven-gifted still an earthly Gift have I!" in his edition of the Goethe-Carlyle correspondence.[9] *Chaos,* the journal edited by Ottilie von Goethe in which a few of Carlyle's poems were first published, is discussed in Reinhard Fink's "Das 'Chaos' und seine Mitarbeiter"[10] and in Trevor D. Jones' "English Contributors to Ottilie von Goethe's 'Chaos,'" where Jones also identified and dated various contributions by British authors, including Carlyle's "Tragedy of the Night-Moth."[11] Leonard Mackall's "Verse von Frau Carlyle unter Goethes Gedichten an Personen" presents the text of and recounts the story of how Carlyle's poem "For th' Heaven-gifted" came to be published as one of Goethe's own poems in the Weimar Edition of Goethe's works.[12]

Froude has already been mentioned for his comments on Carlyle's poetic skills, but his most valuable contribution to the study of Carlyle's poetry stems from the facts that he was Carlyle's own chosen biographer, had access to Carlyle's papers, and spent considerable time with Carlyle himself. Shoddy though his editorial practices may be by current standards, one is still indebted to Froude for his printings of poems from manuscripts that have since disappeared or are otherwise presently inaccessible, and especially for his printing of "Oh! Life Turmoil" since it is his printing that has preserved the poem. Similarly, although he is sometimes mistaken, Froude provides quite a number of personal anecdotes and quotations from Carlyle pertaining to his views on the art of poetry and on the biographical circumstances surrounding some of the poems. In addition to the Carlyle poems mentioned above, Froude also prints some of Carlyle's translations and some of Jane's poems as well.

Charles Eliot Norton, who also knew Carlyle and was a friend of Carlyle's niece Mary and nephew Alexander Carlyle, edited two of Carlyle's notebooks and published them as *Two Note Books of Thomas Carlyle from 23d March 1822 to 16th May 1822*. Norton's edition provides the only text for two of the poems that appear in these journals — "The Hildebrands" and "Priest-ridden" — his texts of the other poems from the journals provide more accurate transcription than Froude's printings do, and Norton's texts also describe Carlyle's manuscript revisions where they appear.

Alexander Carlyle was the son of Carlyle's brother Alexander and married Carlyle's niece Mary Aitken, who lived with Carlyle as his housekeeper and secretary from 1868 until his death in 1881. Between them, Mary and Alexander Carlyle were privy to a vast quantity of personal information given by Carlyle himself, and ultimately the bulk of his papers also passed into their ownership, much of it later being edited and published by Alexander Carlyle. In his edition of Thomas and Jane Carlyle's *Love Letters* (II, 341-360) Alexander Carlyle prints texts of poems by both Carlyles along with valuable biographical notes relating to authorship and dating for these and other Carlyle poems.

ii

Biographical and Historical Contexts

The story of Carlyle's life has been told in detail many times before, and it is not our intention to repeat it here. However, most of his poems are apprentice and occasional compositions, and therefore some sketch of the contexts from which the poems emerged seems appropriate.

In the village of Ecclefechan where he was born, Carlyle received his elementary education before he was sent to Annan Academy in 1806; and from Annan, he went to the University of Edinburgh in 1809, where he completed the normal arts curriculum in 1813. In 1814 he began Divinity Hall studies at the University as preparation for the ministry. He chose the option of becoming a rural divinity student, having only to present an independently prepared sermon once a year for six years in order to obtain ordination and church appointment;[13] so he was able to leave the University in May, 1814, to begin teaching mathematics at Annan Academy. In 1816 when Carlyle resigned his position in Annan and began teaching in Kirkcaldy as a rival schoolmaster to Edward Irving, the move was an important one in his career. Carlyle had met Irving in 1815 when Irving was already showing promise of becoming a brilliant preacher, but in the two years that they were associated in Kirkcaldy,. a deep - and enduring friendship grew between the two men, and Irving became Carlyle's first real mentor and benefactor.

Carlyle ended his Divinity Hall connection in 1817, and in 1818 Irving and Carlyle both resigned their posts in Kirkcaldy and moved to Edinburgh, where Carlyle's career as a man of letters began in earnest. Between 1820 and 1823 he wrote some twenty articles for David Brewster's *Edinburgh Encylopaedia,* but his main activity was in translating. Carlyle had begun his study of German in 1819,[14] and from 1821-1822 his main public efforts were in translating German works and writing about German literature. The culmination of his interest in German literature came with his *Life of Schiller* — which Irving arranged to have published in the *London Magazine* in 1824 — with his translation of Goethe's *Wilhelm Meister,* also published in 1824, and, in 1827, with the publication of *German Romance* and "Jean Paul Friedrich Richter," Carlyle's first essay in the prestigious *Edinburgh Review.*

More private works were also proceeding apace, and many of them were poems, with the most important poetic catalyst of these years arriving in 1821, when Irving introduced Carlyle to one of his former students, Jane Baillie Welsh. Carlyle began a courtship that continued for the next five years, and part of the courtship entailed Carlyle's efforts to acquaint Miss Welsh with German literature and included his suggestions of various literary projects to be undertaken in concert, including the writing of poems on the same subjects. In addition, of course, independent love poems emerged in the course of the courtship, and even after the courtship was over, Jane continued to be a source of poetic inspiration to Carlyle, as he wrote other poems for her sporadically until the late 1840s. Carlyle's courtship of Jane was not always a smooth one, however, and Mrs. Welsh had misgivings about Carlyle's future, even after Irving had obtained him a post as tutor to a wealthy family in 1822, thus providing a measure of financial security if not emotional or intellectual satisfaction. Moreover, this was the period of Carlyle's religious crisis described in "The Everlasting No" in *Sartor Resartus,* and the entries from his journal of these years document his various anxieties, as do some of the poems.

Things began to look brighter for Carlyle in 1825. He had resigned his position as tutor in 1824 following the publication of *Wilhelm Meister* and had moved to Hoddam Hill Farm with members of his family in 1825. Carlyle spent a year at Hoddam Hill and later recalled,

> This year I found that I have conquered all my scepticisms, agonising doubtings, fearful wrestlings with the foul and vile and soul-murdering Mud-gods of my Epoch; had escaped, as from a worse than Tartarus, with all its Phlegethons and Stygian quagmires; and was emerging, free in spirit, into the eternal blue of ether, — where blessed be Heaven, I have, for the spiritual part, ever since lived. . . . (*Reminiscences,* II, 179)

Another cause for relief came in October, 1826, when at last Carlyle and Jane Welsh were married and moved to Edinburgh to begin their life together. The respite was brief, though, and in spite of some publishing successes, financial troubles continued to beset the Carlyles and motivated their move in 1828 to Craigenputtoch as an economy measure.

Craigenputtoch, or "Hill-Forest of the Puttocks [hawks]" (*Reminiscences*, I, 87-88), is remote today, but in Carlyle's day it was isolated. Thus in many ways it was a perfect retreat for a writer, especially for a writer who was later to have a "soundproof room" built in his house in London. It was at Craigenputtoch that Carlyle laid the true foundation of his literary success as he produced most of his seminal essays; formed important friendships with other literary figures; and, most importantly, wrote *Sartor Resartus*. Among his lesser known literary productions from the six years at Craigenputtoch are about half of his poems, and several of them share a direct relationship to the Carlyles' life there. The first poems written at Craigenputtoch, however, were occasional verses that Carlyle sent to Goethe in 1829.

Carlyle had first corresponded with Goethe in 1824, when he sent a copy of his translation of *Wilhelm Meister* to him; subsequently the two exchanged letters and parcels containing books, gifts, and occasional poems at intervals until Goethe's death in 1832. Goethe was also probably responsible for the publication of Carlyle's poetry in *Chaos* (the weekly coterie journal edited in Weimar by Goethe's daughter-in-law Ottilie). *Chaos* printed four of his poems, and Carlyle seems to have used the journal as a sort of sounding board for reception of his poems since he subsequently published three of these poems in *Fraser's*. In any case, the sending and publication of the poems may be seen as a small detail in the larger exchange that flourished between Carlyle and Goethe during the Craigenputtoch period.

Another very important association for Carlyle began during these years: that with *Fraser's Magazine for Town and Country*.[15] Although Carlyle had enjoyed earlier successes with his translations of and essays on German literature, the subject was beginning to wear thin for him and for his public by 1830. He had already turned his attention to British literature and society with "Burns" (1828) and "Signs of the Times" (1829) in the *Edinburgh Review*, to which Francis Jeffrey had given him access. But Jeffrey left the *Edinburgh Review* in 1829, and although Carlyle continued occasionally to publish essays in that quarterly, his interests were taking him increasingly into subjects and a mode of literary expression that were not particularly appropriate for the eminent Whig publication.

Carlyle's association with *Fraser's* began when the magazine first appeared in 1830, and was surely the result of Edward Irving's recommendation to the publisher, who wrote to Carlyle and invited him to contribute.[16] The magazine was an immediate success, providing the public with a roisterous miscellany of satire and learning and Carlyle with much needed financial relief as *Fraser's* became his primary public outlet during the Craigenputtoch years. Some of Carlyle's essays that appeared in *Fraser's* were "Thoughts on History," "Biography," "Boswell's *Life of Johnson*," "Count Cagliostro," and "The Diamond Necklace"; in addition, several of his poems made their first British appearance in *Fraser's,* as did his story "Cruthers and Jonson" and the book that no other publisher would undertake to print — *Sartor Resartus.* As it turned out, though, when *Sartor* actually began to appear serially, it was too much even for *Fraser's* readers, and the work met with general cries of derision. A notable exception to the prevailing tone at this time was provided by Ralph Waldo Emerson, who praised the book highly.

Emerson had admired Carlyle's earlier writings, and he had visited the Carlyles at Craigenputtoch in August of 1833. Then, while *Sartor* was being serialized, Emerson began his correspondence with Carlyle that was to continue on and off for the next forty years. Out of their friendship came the widening of Carlyle's audience to include America as Emerson volunteered to undertake American editions of various of Carlyle's works. So it happened that *Sartor Resartus* was first published in book form in Boston in 1836, and Carlyle's essays were also first collected and printed in book form there in 1838 as *Critical and Miscellaneous Essays.*

Carlyle made other friends while he lived at Craigenputtoch, notably John Stuart Mill and Leigh Hunt whom he met when he went to London in 1831 to seek a publisher for *Sartor.* Finally, however, much as it may have helped Carlyle to produce the works that came from these years, the isolation at Craigenputtoch began to tell; and it became increasingly evident that if Carlyle was to find his place in the profession of letters, he would need the stimulus of greater society with other thinkers and writers and freer access to resources of research and publication. In the summer of 1834 the Carlyles moved into the house on Cheyne Row in London that was to be their home for the rest of their lives. Carlyle's fortunes began to improve in London, but the improvement was slow at first, and the royalties that he received from Emerson represented a good part of his literary income during the period when he was writing *The French Revolution*. Pressed for funds, in 1837 he gave the first of his series of lectures that he was to give annually over the next three years. Later in 1837 he published *The French Revolution*, the first of his works to be published with his name, and its appearance marked Carlyle's establishment as a writer of exceptional stature. For the rest of his career his works were concerned primarily with history, biography, and social criticism, and the few poems that survive from the years of his literary eminence are increasingly occasional and ephemeral.

iii

Carlyle's Aesthetics

While specific studies of Carlyle's poetry are few, studies of his general theories of poetry are not. Among the more useful of these general studies are Frederick W. Roe's *Thomas Carlyle as a Critic of Literature*; William Savage Johnson's *Thomas Carlyle: A Study of His Literary Apprenticeship 1814-1831*; Hill Shine's *Carlyle's Fusion of Poetry, History, and Religion by 1834*; Charles Richard Sanders' "Carlyle, Browning, and the Nature of a Poet," "Carlyle and Tennyson," and "Carlyle, Poetry, and the Music of Humanity"; Donald R. Swanson's "Carlyle on the English Romantic Poets," and William R. Thurman's "Carlyle, Browning, and Ruskin on One Purpose of Art."[17] Perhaps the most helpful comprehensive presentations of Carlyle's aesthetic theories, though, are to be found in Roe's *Thomas Carlyle as a Critic of Literature* (pp. 26-45) and in G. B. Tennyson's *Sartor Called Resartus* (pp. 89-98), and we are especially indebted to those discussions in the following summary of the main points of Carlyle's theories.

Carlyle introduced the word *aesthetic* into English in his essay on
Richter in 1827 (Tennyson, p. 89), but he had before then begun to
articulate and to practice the aesthetic theory that he was to follow
and expound throughout his career.   At the heart of his aesthetic
theory — indeed of his whole philosophy — is the conception of reality
that he acquired during his study of German literature.

In his interpretation of German idealism, Carlyle concluded that
ultimate reality is not to be found in the visible world, but in timeless
and universal truths for which natural phenomena can provide but
fragmentary representations.   These highest truths, taken together,
constitute Fichte's "Divine Idea" or Goethe's "Open Secret" of the
universe, and they are discovered intuitively, not through sensory
perception or through logical processes.   Ultimately the "Divine Idea"
is unknowable in its entirety, but man can read portions of it in all
things.   *Man* can read something of these truths, but all *men* cannot:

> To the mass of men this Divine Idea of the world lies hidden:
> yet to discern it, to seize it, and live wholly in it, is the
> condition of all genuine virtue, knowledge, freedom; and the
> end, therefore, of all spiritual effort in every age. ("State
> of German Literature," *Works*, XXVI, 58)

The ability to penetrate the veils of eternity and to discover its under-
lying truths is the first important requirement for the poet, for to
Carlyle "He is a *vates*, a seer; a gift of vision has been given him. Has
life no meanings for him, which another cannot equally decipher;
then he is no poet, and Delphi itself will not make him one" ("Burns,"
Works, XXVI, 272).   Actually this gift of vision is the definitive char-
acteristic of any Carlylean hero, whatever his calling, and in *Heroes
and Hero-Worship* Carlyle writes, "A Hero, as I repeat, has this first
distinction, which indeed we may call first and last, the Alpha and
Omega of his whole Heroism, That he looks through the shows of
things into *Things*" (*Works*, V, 55).

While the "Divine Idea" is eternal and changeless, however, the
forms through which it is made manifest in the material world be-
come outworn and decay as age succeeds to age, with the result that

the forms continue to exist as empty shells which no longer adequately represent the spirit that originally informed them. Thus Carlyle's criticism of contemporary religion and society came from his conviction that government and religious institutions no longer embodied the vital spirit from which they had grown, but continued to exist as hollow and parasitic shells when new living forms were needed that could vigororously represent the eternal truths for the nineteenth century. The hero's function, therefore, is to express the portions of the "Divine Idea" that he had glimpsed, and to express them in terms that *will* answer the needs of his times; for

> whoever may forget this divine mystery, the *Vates*, whether Prophet or Poet, has penetrated into it; is a man sent hither to make it more impressively known to us. That always is his message; he is to reveal that to us, — that sacred mystery which he more than others lives ever present with.
>
> (*Heroes, Works,* V, 80-81)

The poet must therefore present the ideal world, but for Carlyle he must present it in terms of the actual world that his audience inhabits: he must unite the ideal and the actual in his works; and the greatest poets' works succeed, as Goethe's do, because the poetry

> is no reminiscence, but something actually present and before us; no looking back into an antique Fairyland, divided by impassable abysses from the real world as it lies about us and within us; but a looking round upon that real world itself, now rendered holier to our eyes, and once more become a solemn temple, where the spirit of Beauty still dwells, and is still, under new emblems, to be worshipped as of old.
>
> ("State of German Literature," *Works,* XXVI, 65)

Moreover, "since only in Reality lies the essence and foundation of all that was ever fabled, visioned, sung, spoken, or babbled by the human species; and the actual Life of Man includes in it all Revelations, true and false, that have been, are, or are to be" ("Count Cagliostro," *Works,* XXVIII, 249), the poet should choose materials that represent *all* aspects of ideal truths. The point of Carlyle's essay on Count Cagliostro and of his poem on Peter Nimmo, for instance, was that these individuals too represented parts of the "Divine Idea," that "Nature was pleased to produce even such a man, even so, not otherwise" ("Count Cagliostro," *Works,* XXVIII, 317). The true poet thus emerges as one who uses the materials of the natural world to express the transcendent values that he has discovered, and he is a maker in the sense that his use of materials is essentially symbolic or metaphoric as he transforms actuality into representations of higher truths.

An obvious corollary to the poet's mission of shaping actuality into forms that express the eternal verities is Carlyle's insistence on the poet's sincerity, on his lack of affectation. Burns' excellence to Carlyle, for example, was that whatever his shortcomings, Burns sincerely spoke the truth as he knew it:

> Here are no fabulous woes or joys; no hollow fantastic sentimentalities; no wiredrawn refinings, either in thought or feeling: the passion that is traced before us glowed in a living heart; the opinion he utters has risen in his own understanding, and been a light to his own steps. ("Burns," *Works,* XXVI, 267)

On the other hand, Byron fails as a great poet because of a lack of sincerity, and Carlyle asked,

> Are his Harolds and Giaours . . . real men; we mean poetically consistent and conceivable men? Do not these characters, does not the character of their author, which more or less shines through them all, rather appear a thing put on for the occasion; no natural or possible mode of being, but something intended to look much grander than nature?

. . . .

> To our minds there is a taint of this sort, something which
> we should call theatrical, false, affected, in every one of these
> otherwise so powerful pieces. ("Burns," *Works,* XXVI, 269)

Byron's defects are that not only are his materials fantastic, but also
that his own expression of self is untrue as well: he has not given a
faithful image of a human soul struggling to accommodate itself to
the "Divine Idea," and his performance can therefore afford no help-
ful enlightenment for other men. Insincerity is to Carlyle a type of
illusion and thus disqualifies a versifier from consideration as a poet
because it is evidence that his performance is the product of only
his art — not of the whole man — and therefore the artifice represents
only the shell of true poetry.

True poetry, again, is the product of *all* of the poet's faculties
working in concert, and in *Heroes and Hero-Worship* Carlyle stressed
this harmonious spontaneity and defined poetry as *"musical Thought"*
(*Works,* V, 83).[18] Part of the passage that led up to Carlyle's defini-
tion is as follows:

> If your delineation be authentically *musical,* musical not
> in word only, but in heart and substance, in all the thoughts
> and utterances of it, in the whole conception of it, then it
> will be poetical; if not, not. — Musical: how much lies in
> that! A *musical* thought is one spoken by a mind that has
> penetrated into the inmost heart of the thing; detected the
> inmost mystery of it, namely the *melody* that lies in it;
> the inward harmony or coherence which is its soul, whereby
> it exists, and has a right to be, here in this world. (*Heroes,*
> *Works,* V, 83)

Carlyle's conception of art is therefore organic in the sense that the
form of the true work or art is dictated from within, or "As the brief-
est definition, one might say, Forms which *grow* round a substance,
if we rightly understand that, will correspond to the real nature and
purport of it, will be true, good; forms which are consciously *put* round

a substance, bad" (*Heroes, Works,* V, 205). His emphasis is always on the sincere expression of *thought,* and therefore Carlyle could say that Richter was a great poet even though he wrote no verse ("Jean Paul Friedrich Richter Again," *Works,* XXVI, 159). If a poet sees his portion of a truth of existence clearly enough, the appropriate vehicle for expressiing his insight will come spontaneously, and the expression will be poetic, whatever its actual form — verse or prose — might turn out to be. It is the idea that makes the poem, not the poetics — although great verse poems have the distinction of having had appropriately eloquent meter and rhyme grow around their ideas.

His views concerning the nature of the poet and his mission necessarily led Carlyle to the conclusion that the poet's efforts usually cannot be wholly successful. No poet, however great, is privy to the entire truth of existence, for instance, and thus his most inspired works can only hope to express portions of the "Divine Idea." Moreover, since the poet must embody his visions in reality, must utter the unutterable, his expression can only be regarded as a more or less crude representation of the truths that he has discovered: "No man works save under conditions. The sculptor cannot set his own free Thought before us; but his Thought as he could translate it into the stone that was given, and the tools that were given. *Disjecta membra* ["dismembered parts"] are all that we find of any Poet, or of any man" (*Heroes, Works,* V, 110-111). Finally, all poets are not born equal in their capacity for vision, nor are all equally gifted in their skills; and those whose work fails — for whatever reasons — to exhibit the unity of ideal and form that Carlyle sought in poetry are judged to be deficient. Therefore, because they did not meet his standards of organic unity, or wholeness, Carlyle called his own poems "Fractions": they are works that represent something less than completed wholes.

His poems present many of Carlyle's characteristic themes and images, but he felt that his ideas had not found their appropriate form in verse; the form was too often artificial, not an organic outgrowth of the idea. In fact, Carlyle increasingly felt that all traditional modes of poetic expression were inappropriate vehicles of thought for his own time, and because of the moral imperative that he attached to

literature, he urged contemporary poets to write in prose.[19] Poetry
could be a harmless, even beneficial, diversion, but the real work of
the day needed to be done in prose. In a letter of 21 February, 1844,
written to his cousin Alexander McKinnow, Carlyle gave counsel that
was typical of his general advice to poets, both in his public and private
statements, all through his career:

> There can be no harm in amusing your leisure with verses,
> if you find it an amusement; but certainly I would by no
> means recommend you to prosecute it in any way as an
> employment, for in that sense I think it can turn to nothing
> but an obstruction and a disappointment. Verse-writing,
> notwithstanding all the talk you hear about it, is in almost
> all cases a totally idle affair: a man was *not* sent into this
> world to write verses — no! If he finds himself called to
> speak, let him *speak,* manfully, some "words of truth and
> soberness"; and, in general, leave the *singing* and verse mak-
> ing part of it, till the very last extremity, of some inward or
> outward call, drive him irresistibly thither. Nay, in these
> times, I observe there is less and less attention paid to things
> in verse; and serious persons everywhere find themselves
> disposed to hear what a man has to say *the shortest way
> and the directest* — that is to say, disencumbered of rhyme.
> I for my share am well content with *this* tendency of the
> world.[20]

iv
Carlyle's Poetic Practice

Carlyle's own poetry does exemplify many of the characteristics
that his aesthetic theories prescribe for the genre. Whatever his subject
matter might be, his treatment of it typically attempts to exhibit a
facet of transcendent reality through a metaphoric shaping of the
materials of actual existence to present the themes that characterize
all of his other writings.

In poems like "Tragedy of the Night-Moth," "The Beetle," and "To a Swallow," for instance, Carlyle uses these creatures as means of symbolically presenting universal truths of existence by comparing the lesser worlds which they inhabit with the poet's world as both move to the same rhythms of the cosmos. The purpose of such comparisons is almost always to indicate the universality of all experience, the organic unity of all creation, in which the poet and the lesser creatures are representative portions. Similarly, Carlyle's nature poems do not typically present conventional descriptions of nature, but use natural phenomena to embody moral lessons on such topics as the relationship of eternity to time. Time is the vesture behind which eternity is concealed, and the river Orr in "Drumwhirn Bridge," therefore, becomes an apt metaphor for eternity flowing through time in the actual world. Thus, in a sense, almost all of Carlyle's poetry is occasional in that he does not imagine the events that he presents in his poetry, but interprets actual occurrences like a walk to the bridge and shapes them so as metaphorically to embody underlying truths that he discovers.

Carlyle's final imperative is, again, to embody ideal reality, to present aspects of the "Divine Idea" in forms that will reawaken his readers' sense of spiritual life. He saw his mission as a corrective one, and the first necessary step towards a correct interpretation of existence was, for him, the rejection of false appearances of reality. Perhaps the theme that recurs most frequently in his poetry is therefore that of renunciation. For Carlyle the term *renunciation* or *entsagen* meant the sacrifice of one's own individual desires in order to attain higher spritual goals,[21] and the effort carried with it the necessary acceptance of sorrow and suffering that inevitably grew from this thwarting of the self's unappeasable appetite for happiness. The actual world might not be the highest reality, but since it is the physical world that man inhabits, it is real enough to cause all manner of frustration and suffering as one struggles to accommodate himself to the "Divine Idea." Most of Carlyle's poems that present complaints about the bitter experience of life and that look forward to eternity as the place of rest thus reflect his fundamental belief in the duality of man's nature and show the difficulty of subduing the lower part of it. The world

of fashion, for example, may be far beneath the world of Craigenput-
toch on the most ideally important level, but on the level of actual
existence in the material world, it is the world of fashion that is dom-
inant. If man rejects, as he should, the world of ease and wealth in
order to follow more important values, he will doubtless attain greater
ultimate happiness, or blessedness, but he will be unlikely to attain
much material happiness in *this* world. Renunciation, then, can be
equated with the traditional Christian doctrine of self-denial, of un-
complaining acceptance of God's will for man, and it constitutes the
passive half of man's duty. For Carlyle the world is not man's true
home, and he is not placed in it to be happy: he is placed in it to
accept God's will and — as the active half of his duty — to struggle
to make the will of God prevail.

Carlyle's other great theme is thus the gospel of work, for it is
through his deeds that man makes ideal truths manifest in the actual
world and therefore makes the will of God prevail. Work is a primary
duty of man in the world, and Carlyle presents this message in poems
covering a wide range of subjects, including love and nature. His one
surviving poem on a historical subject, "Morgarten," for example, is
an exemplum of this theme as it was through their deeds that the
Swiss mountaineers made the ideal of freedom a reality in their land.
On the most basic level, all of Carlyle's poems — like most of his other
writings — are concerned with the doctrine of work, for they represent
his efforts to transform thoughts into deeds; they are in the truest
Carlylean sense his *works*.

As was mentioned earlier, G. B. Tennyson has noted that, in addi-
tion to Carlyle's characteristic themes, his poetry also exhibits many
of his characteristic images and rhetorical habits ("Poetry," 165-173).
These images and rhetorical patterns continued to appear as vehicles
for Carlyle's ideas long after he had stopped writing in verse because
they were organic forms for his thought, but what he felt was *not*
organic to his thought were the more formal details that customarily
distinguish poetry from prose. Carlyle's creative effort was devoted
to the discovery of new forms for expressing truths about existence;
and although his poetry represents a tentative attempt towards the
articulation of his ideas, he finally judged poetry to be an inadequate

means for expression because the expression was too often artificial. Such a conclusion was not a foregone one, though, and his poetry shows Carlyle attempting to find poetic forms that would effectively embody his insights. He consciously avoided imitating the kinds of poems that were being written by his contemporaries, for instance, and one finds no sonnets, no odes, no "Lines on . . ." among his works, and only a few poems in couplets. That his favorite stanzaic form is a variant of the ballad stanza owes more to his identification of that form with the authentic and primal voice of humanity (as exemplified in Burns, for instance) than to the contemporary fondness for literary ballads: Burns is authentic; most contemporary balladeers, not. Similarly, although he echoes Byron's anapestic meter of "The Destruction of Sennacherib" in "Morgarten," such close resemblances are rare. His most common meter — like that of most poetry in English — is iambic, but he also shows a penchant (perhaps deriving from his study of German) for trochaic meters, as about one-fourth of his poems are in some form of that meter. Many of his lines — whatever meter he uses — are irregular, and it was for this irregularity that most of his contemporaries declared Carlyle to be insensitive to the "music" of poetry. The judgment may be a sound one for the most part, but it is not by any means certain that it is a judgment with which Carlyle would entirely agree since he objected to "the same smooth ding-dong r[h]ythm from the first page to the last" as being evidence of artificiality (*Letters,* II, 250). One should thus perhaps view his metrical irregularity as a part of his attempt to put his aesthetic theories into practice rather than as the result of ineptitude or of carelessness.

Regardless of his intentions, however, Carlyle realized that his poems did not fulfill his ideals of literature. They contained his ideas and the images that could embody them, but his verses lacked the complete union of idea and form that he required of literature. One should recall in this context, however, that Carlyle was dissatisfied not only with his own poetry, but with the poetry of virtually all of his contemporaries as well since he thought that none of it adequately answered the needs of the day. The most important artistic discovery that Carlyle made during his apprenticeship was what his mode of expression (and that of the age as well) should be: he discovered that his métier was to be in prose and that his master works (which, incidentally, he also viewed with some dissatisfaction) would have to be produced in that genre.

v

The Text

1. *Lost or otherwise unavailable manuscripts:* Although manuscript materials survive for the majority of the poems presented in this edition, others have been lost or are privately owned and are not available for study. Carlyle himself was responsible for some lost materials. D. A. Wilson quotes Carlyle as saying that he had burned "all the trash of verses I could lay my hands on" when he returned from his trip to Paris in 1824 (*Carlyle Till Marriage,* p. 356). Such may have been the fate of Carlyle's poems on Napoleon, the Bass Rock, and the Kirk of Durisdeer — all of which are mentioned in letters of 1822, but none of which has been printed or mentioned as surviving among Carlyle's effects.[22] The manuscripts of some poems that were printed were also lost, and Alexander Carlyle writes that the manuscript of "The Wish" had been lost before 1909 (*Love Letters,* II, 349n.); in addition, the manuscript of "Tragedy of the Night-Moth" in Jane's handwriting that was reported to have been preserved in Weimar has since disappeared. Of the papers that were in Alexander Carlyle's possession, not all were given to the National Library of Scotland or sold to institutions at auction; and although the manuscript of "To Jane B. Welsh" was sold at auction in 1932, it was purchased by an individual, and its present whereabouts is unknown.[23] Similarly, no one knows precisely what Carlyle materials Alexander Carlyle retained, but the copy of "To a Swallow Building Under Our Eaves" that was written in Jane Carlyle's handwriting is also untraced, and it is not listed as having been sold at auction; it may therefore have been lost, given away, sold privately, or retained. By far the most important Carlyle materials known to be still in private hands, and presumably those of the Carlyle family, are the four notebooks that comprise the journal that Carlyle kept from 1822 to 1873.

Two of the notebooks were edited and published as *Two Note Books of Thomas Carlyle from 23d March 1822 to 16th May 1832* by Charles Eliot Norton, and Froude included many passages from the later notebooks in his *Life*. Since Alexander Carlyle's death the journal has been inaccessible to scholars, with the single exception of Jacques Cabau, who was allowed to examine the manuscript (but not to quote from it) when he was preparing *Thomas Carylye ou le Prométhée Enchainé* (1968). The manuscripts of the poems from the journals are therefore not available for inspection, and whether or not additional poems exist in the notebooks is unknown.[24]

Other poetry manuscripts probably exist as well — especially if one takes seriously Froude's statement that he found "infinite loose sheets of paper" containing verses among Carlyle's papers (*First Forty Years,* I, 172) — but the efforts of the present editors have failed to discover them.

2. *Editorial principles.* The duty of any editor is to present, as far as is possible, an author's work as the author himself finally intended it to be presented. Since, however, Carlyle's poems exist in a variety of states — some in manuscript only, some in authorized printed texts, some in printed versions claiming differing degrees of authority, and some in manuscript *and* in printed texts (also possessing degrees of authority) — the question of final intention can be a complex one, and different situations require different criteria for answering the question.

For instance, although Dyer writes that the last edition of his works that Carlyle personally supervised through the press was the People's Edition (Dyer, p. 58), the present editors have found no evidence to suggest that Carlyle did, in fact, read and correct proof in any thorough or systematic way for that edition. For this reason it was decided to follow as copy-text for Carlyle's poems and translations included in his collected works the earliest printed text possessing authorial sanction. Any exceptions to this practice are detailed in the notes. If the resulting text does not fully represent Carlyle's final intention with respect to accidentals in all instances, one at least may have greater confidence that it does represent *Carlyle's* intention at some stage, and not that of his publisher's reader or appointed clerk.

For poems that exist only in manuscript one has simply to reproduce the manuscript text as accurately as possible. For poems that exist in manuscript and in printed texts, however, one must decide which exhibits final intention. In cases where a manuscript survives, and the printed text supersedes the manuscript — and was produced under Carlyle's control — the printed version was chosen as copy-text. In cases where manuscripts exist along with printed versions that are not authorially sanctioned or that were not published during Carlyle's lifetime, the manuscript has consistently been chosen as copy-text.

Some of Carlyle's poems exist only in printed texts that were printed after his death, and in cases where the poems were printed by different editors, one must decide whose text to follow. For the poems from Carlyle's journal, Norton's text has consistently been followed where possible since he is generally acknowledged to have been a more careful editor than was Froude. Similarly, Alexander Carlyle's texts have been chosen over Froude's when they both print the same poem. In all such cases, however, substantive variants from the rejected text have been included in the list of variants.

Finally, for poems that exist only in printed texts that were published in Carlyle's liftime but without his supervision, one must be satisfied with the text as it survives.

Further discussion of matters relating to choice of copy-text appears in the textual notes that follow the poems.

3. *Format of this edition.* Each poem is presented in clear text, with the exception of titles for poems that lacked them and of line numbers, both of which have been added. Added titles have been enclosed in square brackets, and all titles have been put in all capital letters as this seems to represent Carlyle's own preference. Carlyle's typography has been reproduced as faithfully as possible, with the exception of his periods following titles and the initial word of first lines being printed in small capitals; both practices have been abandoned.

The apparatus for the poems contains the data described by the Center for Scholarly Editions' Introductory Statement,[25] in the order suggested by G. Thomas Tanselle in "Some Principles for Editorial Apparatus"[26] — with the exception of a list of hyphenizations, which has been omitted since none, other than Carlyle's hyphens, appears in his poems. First a *commentary* is given containing available information that is relevant to the context of the poem's composition. This commentary is followed by the *date of composition,* with externally derived dates being enclosed in square brackets and uncertain dates being followed by a question mark and enclosed in square brackets. The date of composition is followed by statements of *manuscript location, place of first publication, texts consulted* for this edition, and the *copy-text* that was chosen for this edition. For each poem every known manuscript and printed text was consulted, but unless they have some special bearing on the history of a given poem, those printings that were done from an already listed text are not included in the list of works consulted. For the poems that seem to require them, *glosses* of unusual terms and translations of foreign words and phrases follow the statement of copy-text. These glosses are intended primarily as a convenience, and the choice of which terms to gloss was dictated by subjectivity and the availability of information. Following the glosses are the *textual notes* giving information pertaining to copy-text selection, manuscript location, printing history, and rationale for emendation and variant listings.

The list of *emendations* presents first the line citation and the reading from this edition followed by a square bracket; then the source of the emendation or a chronological list of previous editors who have also accepted the emendation is given, each separated by a comma. A semicolon then separates the emendation and source from the rejected copy-text reading. Thus,

1 are] Love Letters, Miller; is

means that this edition has rejected the copy-text reading *is* in line one and has accepted the emended reading *are* that appears in *Love Letters* and in Frank Miller's *The Poets of Dumfriesshire.* With the exception of misspellings (and the typographical details already mentioned), all emendations of copy-text, both of substantives and of accidentals, are reported in the list of emendations.

The list of *variants* gives all substantive variants that appear in any

authoritative text consulted, but it does not list accidentals unless
they can be interpreted as having some substantive significance. Cap-
italization, for example, is usually regarded as belonging with accident-
als; but since a characteristic of Carlyle's style is his frequent use of
capitalization as a device of emphasis, capitalization takes on sub-
stantive significance, and variants in capitalization are therefore in-
cluded in the list of variants. Similarly, when punctuation causes a
change in meaning or emphasis, the variant becomes substantive and
is recorded. The entries in the list of variants give first the line cita-
tion and the reading from this edition, followed by a bracket; then
the variant reading is given and its source or sources, each separated
by a comma and enclosed in parentheses. If more than one variant
reading occurs, they are separated by a semicolon. Following this
scheme,

    18 Friend's] friends' (Froude, Miller); Friends' (*Love Letters*)

means that the reading at line eighteen in this edition is *Friend's* where
Froude and Miller print *friends'*, and *Love Letters* prints *Friends'*.
Finally, all authorial revisions of manuscripts are listed and described
in the list of variants, and editorial punctuation in the listings is en-
closed in square brackets.

    Citations follow the list of variants where necessary to give docu-
mentary and substantive notes for material contained in the com-
mentary.

NOTES

    1.   *A Diary,* ed. H[elen] Allingham and D. Radford (1907; rpt. London:
Macmillan, 1908), p. 211.

    2.   "Carlyles Stellung zur Deutschen Sprache und Literatur," *Anglia,*
22 (1899), 10-342. Carlyle's poetry is discussed on pp. 169-170 and pp. 330-
337.

    3.   *Thomas Carlyle als Künstler* (Göttingen: Göttingen University Press,
1935). Carlyle's poetry is discussed on pp. 44-55 and p. 59.

    4.   Tennyson subsequently printed a slightly different version of one
of the poems, included brief further discussion of Carlyle's poems, and gave
a fairly detailed treatment of "Peter Nimmo" in *Sartor* Called *Resartus,* pp. 60-
65.

5.   *The Carlyle Country* (1904; rpt. New York: Haskell House, 1973), pp. 218-219.

6.   *Thomas Carlyle,* 2nd ed. (London: Marshall Japp, 1881), pp. 229-235.

7.   *The Poets of Dumfriesshire* (Glasgow: James MacLehose, 1910), pp. 252-253. Additional discussion of Carlyle's poetry is found on pp. 243-256.

8.   *Mr. Froude and Carlyle* (New York: Dodd, Mead, 1898), pp. 113-120.

9.   *Goethes Briefwechsel mit Thomas Carlyle* (Dachau: Eihhorn, 1913), p. 72, p. 63 of appendix, and Plate IV respectively.

10.   "Das 'Chaos' und seine Miterbeiter," in *Chaos: Herausgegeben von Ottilie von Goethe unter Einschluss der Fortsetzungen Création und Creation* (Bern: Herbert Lang, 1968), pp. 43-53.

11.   "English Contributors to Ottilie von Goethe's 'Chaos,'" *English Goethe Society,* 9 (1931-1933), 68-91.

12.   "Verse von Frau Carlyle unter Goethes Gedichten an Personen," *Goethe Jahrbuch,* 25 (1904), 234-236.

13.   Edwin W. Marrs, Jr., Introd., *The Letters of Thomas Carlyle to His Brother Alexander,* ed. Edwin W. Marrs, Jr. (Cambridge: Harvard University Press, 1968), p. 10.

14.   For details of Carlyle's study of German see Rodger Tarr and Ian Campbell, "Carlyle's Early Study of German, 1819-21," *Illinois Quarterly,* 34 (1971), 19-27; and John Clubbe, ed. *Two Reminiscences of Thomas Carlyle* (Durham: Duke University Press, 1974), 3-21.

15.   The standard work on *Fraser's* is Miriam Thrall's *Rebellious Fraser's* (New York: Columbia University Press, 1934). We are also indebted to G. B. Tennyson's discussion of *Fraser's* in *Sartor Called Resartus,* pp. 131-141.

16.   *Letters,* V, 80n.; see also Thrall, pp. 33-34.

17.   *Thomas Carlyle as a Critic of Literature* (New York: Columbia University Press, 1910); *Thomas Carlyle: A Study of His Literary Apprenticeship 1814-1831* (1911; rpt. New York: Haskell House, 1971); *Carlyle's Fusion of Poetry, History, and Religion by 1834* (Chapel Hill: University of North Carolina Press, 1938); "Carlyle, Browning, and the Nature of a Poet," *Emory University Quarterly,* 16 (1960), 197-209; "Carlyle and Tennyson," *PMLA,* 76 (1961), 82-97; "Carlyle, Poetry, and the Music of Humanity," *Western Humanities Review,* 16 (1962), 53-66; "Carlyle on the English Romantic Poets," *Lock Haven Review,* 11 (1969), 25-32; "Carlyle, Browning, and Ruskin on One Purpose of Art," *South Atlantic Bulletin,* 37 (1972), 52-57.

18.   For a more detailed discussion of "musical thought" and of Carlyle's views on music and its relation to poetry, see Charles Richard Sanders, "Carlyle, Poetry, and the Music of Humanity," *Western Humanities Review,* 16 (1962), 53-66. Also see Carlyle's letter to Leigh Hunt of 29 October, 1833, in *Letters,* VII, 26-31.

19.   Probably the most celebrated instances of these urgings were Car-
lyle's advice to both Brownings to write in prose and his expressed regrets that
Tennyson was misapplying his talents by writing in verse.   For examples of
Carlyle's statements see respectively Charles Richard Sanders, "Carlyle, Browning,
and the Nature of a Poet," *Emory University Quarterly*, 16 (1960), 197-209
and Carlyle's letters of 30 December, 1847, and 27 January, 1867, to Emerson
in *The Correspondence of Emerson and Carlyle*, ed. Joseph Slater (New York:
Columbia University Press, 1964), pp. 436-437 and 552-553.

20.   New York *Daily Tribune*, 24 February, 1847, p. 2, col. 1.

21.   For a more detailed discussion of Carlyle's conception of *renuncia-
tion* see Charles Frederick Harrold, *Carlyle and German Thought: 1819-1834*
(New Haven: Yale University Press, 1934), pp. 314-330.

22.   The letters in which these poems are mentioned are Carlyle's letter
to Jane of about 17 May and her response (Napoleon), Jane's letter of 1 July
to Carlyle (Bass Rock), and Carlyle's letter to Jane of 11 September (Kirk);
the passages can be found in *Letters*, II, 109, 114, 143; and 162 respectively.

Some lines on Napoleon did appear in "Illudo Chartis," Carlyle's unfinished
manuscript, but the manuscript itself was removed from the Carlyle house in
London in about 1960, and its present location is not known.   The manuscript
was printed by Marjorie P. King in "'Illudo Chartis': An Initial Study of Car-
lyle's Mode of Composition," *Modern Language Review*, 49 (1954), 164-175.
The lines on Napoleon are given in King's text as

> "I will now sing of that mighty Beast
> Whon [sic] the river Siene [sic] that stays,
> Who proudly raiseth up his crest,
> And many men he often slays." (p. 165)

23.   Sotheby's Catalogue, p. 25, item 151.   At the same auction a
wrought-iron necklace that Goethe had given the Carlyles was also sold, along
with a manuscript of what the catalogue lists as unprinted verses by both Thomas
and Jane Carlyle on the subject of the necklace (p. 50, item 280).   The present
owner of the necklace was kind enough to send the editors copies of the verses,
and Carlyle's are his translation of the poem that Goethe sent with the neck-
lace in 1827, not original verses of Carlyle's; see ["Dark Chain"] in this edition.

24.   For a discussion of the history of the journal after Alexander Car-
lyle's death, see Ian Campbell, "James Barrett and Carlyle's 'Journal,'" *N&Q,*
215, no. 1 (1970), 19-21.   The situation with respect to the journal's access-
ibility may have altered somewhat recently, however; see the textual note to
"Thirty-nine English Articles" in this edition.

25.   *An Introductory Statement* (New York: Modern Language Associa-
tion of America, 1977), p. 3.

26.   *Studies in Bibliography*, 25 (1972), 41-88.

Abbreviations

Barrett — J. A. S. Barrett, whose brief descriptions of the MSS of the poems are found in the Beinecke Library, Yale University. Barrett, a Scot, was an intimate of Alexander Carlyle's, and presumably a part of his information is from Alexander himself.

Carlyle, Alexander — Alexander Carlyle was Carlyle's nephew and until his death retained the bulk of the Carlyle MSS, including the Journal.

Dyer, Isaac W. — *A Bibliography of Thomas Carlyle's Writings and Ana.* Portland, Maine: The Southworth Press, 1928.

Essays — *Critical and Miscellaneous Essays.* 1st ed. 4 vols. Boston: James Munroe, 1838-1839. 2nd ed. London: James Fraser, 1840.

Fielding — K. J. Fielding, "Unpublished Manuscripts — II: Carlyle's Scenario for *Cromwell*," *Carlyle Newsletter,* no. 2 (March, 1980), 6-13.

"Fractions" — The title that Carlyle gave to the appended writings in Vol. I of *Critical and Miscellaneous Essays*; the seven poems published in his *Essays* make up the bulk of the "Fractions."

Froude — James A. Froude, *Thomas Carlyle: A History of the First Forty Years of His Life, 1795-1835.* 2 vols. London: Longmans, Green & Co., 1882. *Thomas Carlyle: A History of His Life in London, 1834-1881.* 2 vols. London: Longmans, Green & Co., 1884. John Clubbe, abridged edition. Columbus: Ohio State University Press, 1979.

Letters — *The Collected Letters of Thomas and Jane Welsh Carlyle.* 9 vols. Duke-Edinburgh Edition. Ed. Charles Richard Sanders and K. J. Fielding. Durham, North Carolina: Duke University Press, 1970—.

Love Letters — *The Love Letters of Thomas Carlyle and Jane Welsh.* 2 vols. Ed. Alexander Carlyle. London: John Lane, 1909.

Masson — David Masson, *Edinburgh Sketches and Memories.* London: Adam and Charles Black, 1892.

Miller — Frank Miller, *The Poets of Dumfriesshire.* Glasgow: Macklehose, 1910.

Nicoll — H. J. Nicoll, *Thomas Carlyle.* Edinburgh: Macniven & Wallace, 1881.

Original Reviews — *Original Reviews, mostly of German Literature, contributed to the Edinburgh Review, the Foreign Review, and Fraser* [sic] *between the years 1827 and 1833.* A bound volume of reviews presented to Jane Carlyle by Thomas: Beinecke Library.

Reminiscences — *Reminiscences.* Ed. Charles Eliot Norton. 2 vols. London: Macmillan and Co., 1887.

Shepherd — Richard H. Shepherd, *Memoirs of the Life and Writings of Thomas Carlyle.* 2 vols. London: W. H. Allen, 1881.

Sotheby's Catalogue — *Catalogue of Printed Books, Autograph Letters, Literary Manuscripts. Oil Paintings, Drawings & Engravings, Works of Art, China, Furniture, &c. formerly the Property of Thomas Carlyle, 1795-1881, and Now Sold by Order of the Executors of His Nephew, Alexander Carlyle.* London: J. Davy, 1932. Sale date: 13-14 June.

Tennyson — G. B. Tennyson, "Carlyle's Poetry to 1840: A Checklist and Discussion, a New Attribution, and Six Unpublished Poems," *Victorian Poetry,* 1 (1963), 161-181. *Sartor* Called *Resartus.* Princeton, New Jersey: Princeton University Press, 1965.

Two Note Books — *Two Note Books of Thomas Carlyle from 23d March 1822 to 16th May 1832.* Ed. Charles Eliot Norton. New York: Grolier Club, 1898.

Wilson — David A. Wilson, *Carlyle Till Marriage (1795-1826).* London: Kegan Paul, 1923. *Carlyle to "The French Revolution" (1826-1837).* London: Kegan Paul, 1924.

Works — Centenary Edition. Ed. H. D. Traill. 30 vols. London: Chapman and Hall, 1896-1899.

Wylie — William H. Wylie, *Thomas Carlyle, The Man and His Books.* London: Marshall Japp, 1881.

Chronology
(Poems are marked with an asterisk)

1795 Thomas Carlyle born in the Arched House in Ecclefechan, 4 December

1798 Family moves into a cottage in Ecclefechan

1801 Jane Baillie Welsh born in Haddington, 14 July

1802 Carlyle begins formal elementary education in Ecclefechan

1806-09 Attends Annan Academy

1809-13 Attends University of Edinburgh

1814-16 Mathematics teacher at Annan Academy; Preaches sermon, "Before I Was Afflicted I Went Astray" (1814)

1815 Carlyle family moves to Mainhill Farm; Carlyle preaches sermon, "Num detur religio naturalis" [Is There a Natural Religion?]; Carlyle meets Edward Irving
* "The Rival Brothers" [Jane]

1816-18 Schoolmaster in Kirkcaldy;
* "My Loved Minstrel" 1816 [Jane]

1817 Carlyle gives up ministry;
* "Tragedy of the Night-Moth" 1817-22?

1818 Carlyle meets Margaret Gordon; Moves to Edinburgh;
* "Peter Nimmo" 1818-30?

1819 Carlyle begins study of German; Translates scientific works for Edinburgh *Philosophical Journal*; Studies law briefly

1820-23 Writes twenty articles for Dr. David Brewster's *Edinburgh Encyclopaedia*

1821 Carlyle meets Jane Baillie Welsh, May; Publishes a review of Joanna Baille's *Metrical Legends* in *New Edinburgh Review,* his first original essay

1822 Irving obtains Carlyle a position as tutor to the Charles Buller family, his first financial security; Publishes first article on German literature, a review of a translation of

Goethe's *Faust*, in *New Edinburgh Review;*
* "The Fisher" [both] ;
* "The Wish" [Carlyle] ;
* "An Indian Mother's Lament" [Jane] ;
* "A Love Song" [Jane] ;
* "From East to West" [Jane] ;
* "I Love the Mountain Torrent" [Jane] ;
* "The Wish" [Jane] ;
* "Lines to Lord Byron" [Jane] ;
* "Verses Written at Midnight" [Jane] ;
Carlyle finishes translation of Legendre's *Elements of Geometry* for Brewster (published in 1824 with Brewster's name); Leith Walk "Everlasting No" experience;
* "With the Bramah's Pen";
* "Morgarten";
* "Faust's Curse";
"Cruthers and Jonson";
* "Lines on — I Don't Know What"? [Jane] ;
* "The Setting Sun"? [Jane] ;
* "With Song and Dance Grotesque"? [Jane]

1823   Carlyle begins biography of Schiller and translation of Goethe's *Wilhelm Meisters Lehrjahre;*
* "Who Never Ate His Bread in Sorrow";
* "Now Fare Thee Well";
* "They Chide Thee"?
* "Where Shall I Find Thee?" 1823-25?

1824   * "Confessio Fidei";
Schiller published serially in *London Magazine;*   First visit to London;
*   *Wilhelm Meister* published, containing "Who Never Ate His Bread in Sorrow" and "Where Lemon-Trees Do Bloom";
Resigns position with the Bullers; Trip to Paris

1825   *Schiller* published in book form; Moves to Hoddam Hill;
* "To Jane B. Welsh";
* ["The Village" published in *Dumfries Monthly Magazine;*

* "Thunder-Storm" puslished in *Dumfries Monthly Magazine;*
* "Illudo Chartis" 1825-26?
1826 * "Thunder Storm" published in *Dumfries Monthly Magazine;*
* "The Sower's Song";
Family moves to Scotsbrig; Carlyle and Jane Welsh Marry, 17 October;
* "Cui Bono"?
1827 * [*German Romance* published, containing "Enweri Tells Us" and "For the Tie Is Snapt Asunder";
* "The Hildebrands";
Carlyle's first essay published in *Edinburgh Review,* "Jean Paul Friedrich Richter"; "State of German Literature" published in *Edinburgh Review;* Candidate for chairs at University of St. Andrews and University of London, fails both;
* "Dark Chain"? [both]
1828 Move to Craigenputtoch, May; "Burns" published in *Edinburgh Review;*
* "My Own Four Walls" 1828-30?
1829 "Signs of the Times" published in *Edinburgh Review;*
* "Scotland Prides";
* "To the Poet"
1830 "Jean Paul Friedrich Richter Again" published in *Foreign Review;*
* "The Sigh";
* "O Time";
Death of Carlyle's sister Margaret, 22 June;
* "Thy Quiet Goodness";
* "Cui Bono" published in *Chaos* and in *Fraser's;*
* "Faust's Curse" published in *Chaos;*
* "Tragedy of the Night-Moth" published in *Chaos;*
* "The Sower's Song" published in *Chaos;*
* "The Wandering Spirits";
* "The Beetle";

Carlyle begins *Sartor Resartus*, by end of October;
"Thoughts on History" published in *Fraser's*;
* "Nay, This Is Hope" [Jane]

1831 * "The Beetle," "Peter Nimmo," and "The Osculation of the Stars" published in *Fraser's*; "Taylor's Historic Survey of German Poetry" published in *Edinburgh Review*;
* "The Sower's Song" published in *Fraser's*;
* "For the Poet," published later in the year in *Chaos*;
"The Nibelungen Lied" published in *Westminster Review*;
Completes *Sartor Resartus,* July; Leaves for London to seek publisher for *Sartor,* 4 August;

1831 * "Tragedy of the Night-Moth" published in *Fraser's*;
* "Priest-Ridden";
"Characteristics" published in *Edinburgh Review*;
* "Absent"?

1832 Death of Goethe, 22 March; "Biography" published in *Fraser's*; "Boswell's *Life of Johnson*" published in *Fraser's*;
* "Oh! Life Turmoil";
* "Drumwhirn Bridge"

1833 "Count Cagliostro" published in *Fraser's*;
Emerson visits Craigenputtoch, 25-26 August;
* "Crichope Linn";
* "An Hannchen";
Sartor Resartus published serially in *Fraser's,* November 1833-August 1834;
* "Adieu"?
* "Today"?
* "Fortuna"?

1834 Jeffrey refuses to recommend Carlyle for chairs at University of Edinburgh;
* "To a Swallow";
Move to Chelsea, June; Carlyle begins *The French Revolution*;
* "Drumwhirn Bridge" published in *Leigh Hunt's London Journal*;
* "The Wish" [Carlyle] published in *Leigh Hunt's London Journal*; Death of Edward Irving, 7 December

1835   Carlyle meets John Sterling;
        * "Thirty-nine English Articles"
1836   *Sartor Resartus* publshed in book form, Boston
1837   "The Diamond Necklace" published in *Fraser's*; Lectures
        on German Literature; *The French Revolution* published
1838   "Sir Walter Scott" published in *London and Westminster
        Review*;   Lectures on History of European Literature; First
        British edition of *Sartor Resartus*; *Critical and Miscellaneous
        Essays* published, Boston;
        * three "Songs" 1838-40?
        * "What Is Heaven"?
1839   Lectures on Revolutions of Modern Europe; "Chartism"
        published
1840   Second edition of *Essays,* London; Lectures on Heroes and
        Hero-Worship.
1841   *Heroes and Hero-Worship* published;
        * "Cock-a-doodle-doo"
        * "The Lasses of the Canongate"
1842   * "Gae 'Wa Wi"
1843   *   *Past and Present* published, containing "The Builder of
        This Universe" and "Mason-Lodge"
1845   *Oliver Cromwell's Letters and Speeches* published
1847   * "Unused to Trade"
1848   * "Dirge: 'Fear no More'"
1849   * "Simon Brodie";
        * "Einsam, Einsam";
        "Occasional Discourse on the Nigger Question" published
        in *Fraser's*
1850   *Latter-Day Pamphlets* published
1851   *Life of John Sterling* published
1853   Death of Carlyle's mother, 25 December
1858-65 *Frederick the Great* published
1863   * "Ilias (Americana) in Nuce"
1866   Inaugural address at University of Edinburgh;
        * "The Nightingale";
        Death of Jane Carlyle, 21 April;
        * "O Busk Ye"

The Poems of Thomas Carlyle

1
TRAGEDY OF THE NIGHT-MOTH

Magna ausus

'Tis placid midnight, stars are keeping
  Their meek and silent course in heaven;
Save pale recluse, for knowledge seeking,
  All mortal things to sleep are given.

But see! a wandering Night-moth enters,   5
  Allured by taper gleaming bright;
A while keeps hovering round, then ventures
  On Goethe's mystic page to light.

With awe she views the candle blazing;
  A universe of fire it seems   10
To moth-*savante* with rapture gazing,
  Or Fount whence Life and Motion streams.

What passions in her small heart whirling,
  Hopes boundless, adoration, dread;
At length her tiny pinions twirling,   15
  She darts and — puff! — the moth is dead!

The sullen flame, for her scarce sparkling,
  Gives but one hiss, one fitful glare;
Now bright and busy, now all darkling,
  She snaps and fades to empty air.   20

Her bright gray form that spread so slimly,
    Some fan she seemed of pigmy Queen;
Her silky cloak that lay so trimly,
    Her wee, wee eyes that looked so keen,

Last moment here, now gone for ever,   25
    To nought are passed with fiery pain;
And ages circling round shall never
    Give to this creature shape again!

Poor moth! near weeping I lament thee,
    Thy glossy form, thy instant wo;   30
'Twas zeal for 'things too high' that sent thee
    From cheery earth to shades below.

Short speck of boundless Space was needed
    For home, for kingdom, world to thee!
Where passed unheeding as unheeded,   35
    Thy little life from sorrow free.

But syren hopes from out thy dwelling
    Enticed thee, bade thee earth explore, —
Thy frame so late with rapture swelling,
    Is swept from earth forevermore!   40

Poor moth! thy fate my own resembles:
    Me too a restless asking mind
Hath sent on far and weary rambles,
    To seek the good I ne'er shall find.

Like thee, with common lot contented,　　45
　　With humble joys and vulgar fate,
I might have lived and ne'er lamented,
　　Moth of a larger size, a longer date!

But Nature's majesty unveiling
　　What seem'd her wildest, grandest charms,　　50
Eternal Truth and Beauty hailing,
　　Like thee, I rushed into her arms.

What gained we, little moth? Thy ashes,
　　Thy one brief parting pang may show:
And thoughts like these, for soul that dashes　　55
　　From deep to deep, are — death more slow!

2
PETER NIMMO

RHAPSODY
Numeris fertur lege solutis

Old Boece, in jail, did with a certain pathos
Write on *Consolation*; the *scribendi cacoethes*
Serv'd his turn: so shall it mine this rainy day,
Be it neither man nor woman heed my lay.
Praise to Cadmus! that from those same old Phenicians   5
He brought alphabetic Letters fro his Theban Grecians;
And from Grecian to the Scottish! The most sovereign thing
For all Sciences, and sedentary men that preach or sing!
Hereby Time and Space, our foes, if not annihilated
Are laid on their beam-ends, lam'd, and quite prostrated: 10
Art thou lonely, idle; friendless, toolless, nigh distract;
Hand in bosom; jaw, except for chewing, ceased to act?
Matters not, so thou have ink, and see the Why and How;
Drops of Copperas dye make There a Here, and Then a Now.
Must the brain lie fallow, simply since it is alone?   15
And the heart, in heaths and splashy weather, turn to stone?
Shall a living Man be mute as twice-sold mackerel?
If not speaking, if not acting, I can write — in doggerel.
For a subject? Earth is wonder-fill'd; for instance, Peter
                                 Nimmo:
Think of Peter's "being's myst'ry": I will sing of him O!   20
Universe (so thou have time) attend my rhyming,
Sense with sound, on meekest theme, correctly chiming!

TO PETER NIMMO

I

Thrice-lov'd Nimmo! are thou still, in spite of Fate,
Footing those cold pavements; void of meal and mutton;
To and from that everlasting College-gate;   25
With thy blue hook-nose, and ink-horn hung on button?

Always have I noted that long simple nose of thine
How it droops most meekly over shallowest chin,
Ever-smiling lips with scarcely-squinting eyes does join:
Fittest bush for the "mild penny-wheep" is sold within!   30

Soot-brown coat, I know, is button'd, and thy motion
To all class-rooms is a short, half-hurried trudge:
Peter! is there, was there, any fact or notion
In that porous head of thine one night will lodge?

No one! Simplest Peter, wilt thou never know   35
That thy brain is made of substance adipose?
Whilst thou beat'st and heat'st it, all to oil does go:
Cease, fond struggling man, what bootless toils are those!

Canst thou τιμή yet decline, or know the gender
(On thy oath) of a neuter from a feminine?   40
Peter, no! Thou know'st it not, thou vain pretender:
Met the Sun's eye ever so strange a case as thine?

For 'tis twenty years and five since thou art seen
In all Class-rooms, Lectures, thou unweari'd biped,
List'ning, prying, jotting, with an eye so mildly keen: 45
And what boots it? Vain were ev'n the Delphic Tripod.

Danaus' Daughters had a water-sieve to fill;
Fate like thine poor Nimmo, yet in other guise:
Thee no Fear doth urge, but Hope and readiest will;
Hope that springs eternal, Hope of being wise!   50

II

'Tis said that once, ere manhood's prime began,
My Peter, journeying thro' some mountain pass,
'Gan meditate upon Life's mazy plan:
He had leisure for't, being mounted on an Ass.

'Twas summer sabbath-day, the Ass went slow: 55
Rose wondrous, silent hills, beneath blue sky;
From time to time in valley far below
The little Kirk, on verdant knoll, attracts his eye.

Dark lay the world in Peter's labouring breast:
Here was he (words of import strange); *He* here!   60
Mysterious Peter, on mysterious hest:
But Whence? How? Whither? nowise will appear.

What *was* this marv'lous Universe at all?
Some painted diving-bell in Chaos-Ocean?   65
Poor oysters we in dredge of Starry Ball?
And cries the Belly: Peter, *my* Promotion?

Musing these mighty topics, Peter's mind
In vortex dark from side to side did tumble;
Like drifting tub, "fix'd point" nowhere could find
But, sport of waves, amid the sea-wreck, jumble.   70

Seem'd nothing clear on Earth save trot of Cuddy;
That steadiest trot yclept of "butter-and-eggs",
Which patters on, in roadway dry or muddy,
Nought heeding halter, heel, or dangling legs.

As thus the Ass and Peter on did work,   75
The Ass jogtrotting, Peter in brown-study,
His eye (Peter's) glanced on the little Kirk;
The doors flew open: Peter stopt his Cuddy.

Forth rush'd a tide of shepherd-dogs, and then
Of shepherd-people, simple hearers there;   80
With hum of greetings scatter o'er the glen,
Each on his path, or climb the mountains bare.

Soon stands the Kirk alone among its tombs,
But Peter gazes on it for a space;
The scene had struck like "blue-bore" thro' his glooms,   85
And sunlit now, he sees both goal and race.

Warm love in floods thro' Peter's bowels flows,
With hand and *un*arm'd heel he wakes his beast,
And (tears in eyes, and one on point of nose)
Forth-jogging says: God bids me be a Priest!   90

O Peter, what an hour of heavenly knowledge,
Birth-hour of thy whole wondrous destiny!
Thou trottedst on, to grammar school, to College,
Where still thou trottest — with what speed we see.

III

And yet what a joy is thine, O Peter,   95
    The joy to be ever learning!
No lips of a maiden love are sweeter
    Than light on Truth's first morning.

And dwellest thou not in that soul's aurora
    The Gates of the East thy station?   100
No shadows behind, clear sheen before thee
    A hop'd, not come, Revelation!

Thou rather, as Poets deign of Apollo,
    Bright Young-one (graybearded, ragged)
The wheels of the Sun dost ever follow   105
    (Not driving indeed, yet dragged).

IV

Where Peter lodges? How his pot doth boil?
This truly knoweth, guesseth no man:
He spins not, neither does he toil,
Lives free as ancient Greek or Roman.   110

Some think on perfumes he is fed
Like that bright Bird of Araby;
And being a Phoenix-fowl, for bed
Doth roost at night on forest tree.

Vain talk! some earthly food he seeks,   115
As well as spiritual food and culture:
Myself have seen him eat beef-steaks,
Nay bolt, with appetite of vulture.

Or art thou, Peter, that old wand'ring Jew
(Good Lord!) in new shape come again? —   120
Pshaw! Look in's face so parboiled, dusky-blue,
Yet patient, glad! — suspicion false and vain!

Where lodges he! Hath not the Crow a nest?
Fit fodder groweth for all beasts and men:
He lodges where he finds it readiest   125
And feeds full oft the Lord knows how or when.

                        V

At midnight hour did Peter come,
Right well I knew his tap and tread;
With smiles I placed two pints of rum
Before him, and one cold sheephead.   130

How joy'd thy soul at sight of prog,
With wind thy belly long kept full!
Like reek, went glass on glass of grog,
Snick-snack, the sheephead is a *skull*!

And then O Peter what a gabble: 135
High birth, preferments, and so forth,
Thy race known since the Tower of Babel,

Those fam'd "Black Nimmos of the North"!

Should College honours from thee fly,
As Envy follows most the great,   140
Thou hadst an Earldom cut and dry,
In House of Peers couldst take thy seat.

There too wouldst think upon us all,
Wouldst be a friend without a marrow —
Good soul! He from his chair did fall   145
Dead-drunk: I sent him off in barrow.

Thus, solv'd in sheephead-juice and rum,
That soul's whole secret you might see:
His Essence (in strange menstruum),
Like yours and mine, was — *Vanity.*   150

VI

L'Envoy

Who is mad without a peer?
Madder still from year to year?
Peter 'tis, I fear:
Sure 'tis Peter, sure 'tis Peter,
Life's a variorum.   155

Who is wise as Swift or Pope?
Arrow-straight his way doth grope?
Peter 'tis, I hope:
Sure 'tis Peter, sure, &c.

Who is like all sons of men? 160
On addle eggs a hatching hen?
Peter 'tis, I ken:
Sure 'tis Peter, sure 'tis Peter,
Life's a variorum.

3
The Wish

How oft the gen'rous with the selfish mated,
    Must drag in lonesomeness a galling chain!
How oft the two that might have lov'd are fated
    Never to meet, or soon to part again!

Yet here — while in earth's wilderness we linger,   5
    Desponding, sick at heart, unnerv'd in hand,
Young Hope by times will point with cherub finger
    To spots of verdure in that "weary land."

Some shadow of the good we're blindly seeking,
    Some scene of peace — some maid we might adore, 10
Will thrill — like music of his far home, meeting
    The exile on a friendless foreign shore.

With sighs one asks — O! might not, could not I,
    From heartless bustle, dungeon-gloom of town,
With *her* to love me best, for ever fly, —   15
    'Mid still retirements, make my soul *my own?*

In sunny vales calm homes arise for many;
    The sky, the earth, their glad looks spread for all;
And may not friendship's balm be wish'd by any
    Whose heart is true, and beats at friendship's call? 20

Each chain'd to th' oar by thousand imag'd wants,
    See Fashion's galley-slaves and Mammon's ply;

Not theirs the bliss love earn'd by virtue grants —
    By lofty aims and deeds that may not die!

Their wages, gilded straws, for ever leaving,   25
    Might not *one* kindred pair go hand in hand —
The heart's joy with the mind's light interweaving —
    To wisdom's haunts, to fancy's fairy land?

Th' undying minds of ev'ry age around us, —
    The world's, our being's mystery to view —   30
If in us dwelt some thoughts might live beyond us,
    To form them, find them, hearers "fit tho' few."

In tasks like these were not enough to do?
    In other's arms were not enough to feel?
Clear as the summer sun our days might flow,   35
    And bright their end be like that sun's farewell.

Vain longings! vain! No pow'r will hear me,
    To darkness fades my baseless dream;
No bosom-friend or home must cheer me,
Low toil, pale care sit mocking near me,   40
    My past, my future mates they seem.

A kingly thought with a captive's fate
    Wasteth the heart to misery driven:
But to steadfast men in their low estate,
By stern endeavourings, minds elate,   45
    To light the gloom of life is given.

And noble 'tis, without complaining,
    Our lot to suffer, task fulfil,
Thro' scowls, neglect, and chill disdaining,
In pain — alone — our pride retaining,   50
    Untir'd work out our purpos'd will.

Be calm'd, my soul! No act of thine
    With fame can gild thy dreary doom;
But whoso walks firm duty's line
'Mid life's sick mists unstain'd may shine,   55
    And — sound is the sleep of the tomb.

4
WITH THE BRAMAH'S PEN

If pens could feel like men, few men I ween
    Were glad as thou — poor pen of Bramah!
To think what must be and what might have been
    The tenor of their life's small drama.

How oft a pen all clear as thou has graced   5
    The choppy fist of Scotch compiler;
The lies of Faction or Chicane has traced
    With Lawyer pens or hired Reviler;

In rustic Manse in parson's ink has pin'd,
    Seen nought but sermons, punch, backgammon;   10
With dandy clerk or bloated cit confined,
    Like him been ever drudge to Mammon!

Now mark the fate I give thee lucky Steel,
    Prefer'd how far to all thy brothers!
The pressure of my Jane's soft hand to feel,   15
    Still hers to be and ne'er another's.

No cold ignoble thought is thine to write,
    No word from crooked purpose flowing;
But dictates of a lofty spirit pure and bright
    For Good and Great with fervour glowing.   20

And thine it may be, if thy Mistress will,
    To mark some high and hallow'd pages,

Which stamp'd with genius, shrined on Fame's steep hill,
  Shall live with men thro' unborn ages.

So fair a fate, thy fears and perils past   25
  Hast thou, if Jane her favour grant thee;
And happy I, if holding thee, she cast
  One thought on him the Friend that sent thee.

5
MORGARTEN

Proud Hapsburg came forth in the gloom of his wrath,
With his banners of pomp and his Ritters in mail;
For the herdsmen of Uri have fronted his path
And the standard of freedom is raised in their vale.

All scornful advancing he thought as he came   5
How the peasants would shrink at the glance of his eye,
How their heath-cover'd *chalets* in ruin must flame,
And the hopes of the Nations must wither and die.

But mark'd he the moment when thund'ring and vast
The stern voice of the Switzers in echoes arose?   10
When the rocks of their glen from the hill-summits cast
Carried vengeance and death on the heads of their foes?

Now charge in your fury ye sons of the fell,
Now plunge ye your blades in the hearts of his men!
If ye conquer, all times of your glory shall tell;   15
And conquer'd, ye ne'er shall arouse ye again.

Tis done — and the spoilers are crush'd and o'erthrown,
And terror has struck thro' the souls of the proud;
For the Despot of Austria stoops from his throne,
And the war-cry of Uri is wrathful and loud.   20

In speed they came on, but still faster they go,
While ruin and Horror around them are hurl'd:
And the field of Morgarten in splendor shall glow
Like Marathon's field to the end of the world.

6
[THEY CHIDE THEE, FAIR AND FERVID ONE]

They chide thee, fair and fervid one,
 At glory's goal for aiming:
Does not Jove's bird, its flight begun,
Soar up against the beaming Sun,
 Undazed, in splendour flaming?   5

Young brilliant creature, even so
 A lofty instinct draws thee:
Heaven's fires within thy bosom glow,
Could Earth's vain fading vulgar show
 One hour's contentment cause thee?   10

The gay saloon thine *were* to tread,
 Its stateliest scenes adorning;
Thine *be*, by nobler wishes led,
With bays to crown thy lofty head
 All meaner homage scorning.   15

Bright maid! thy gen'rous destiny I view,
 Unutter'd thoughts come o'er me;
Enroll'd 'mong Earth's elected few,
Lovely as morning, pure as dew,
 Thy image stands before me.   20

O! that on fame's far-shining peak,
 With great and mighty number'd.
Unfading laurels I could seek;
This longing spirit then might speak
 The thoughts within that slumber'd.   25

The Sigh.

O sigh not so, my fond and faithful wife,
In sad remembrance, or in boding fear:
This is not Life, this phantasm Type of Life,
What is there to rejoice or mourn for here?

Be it, no wealth, nor fame, nor post is ours,
Small blessedness for infinite Desire:
But has the King his wish in Windsor Towers?
Or but the common lot:— meat, clothes, and fire?

Lone stands our Home amid the sullen moor,
Its threshold by few friends, but beloved;
Yet we are here, we two, still true, tho' poor,
And this too is the World — the "City" of God"!

O'erhangs us not th' Infinitude of Sky,
Where all the starry lights so clear and shine?
Does not that Universe within us lie,
And more,— its maker, or itself divine?

And we, my Love, Life's waking Dream once done
Shall sleep (to waken) leant on other's breast,
And all we loved and toiled for, one by one,
Shall join us there, and wearied be at rest!

Then sigh not so, my fond and faithful wife,
But striving well, have hope, be of good cheer.
Not Rest but worthy Labour is the soul of Life;
Not that, but this, is to be hoped and wish'd for here.

                                    29th January, 1830

O! in the battle's wildest swell,
    By hero's deeds to win thee!
To meet the charge, the stormy yell,
Th' artill'ry's flash, its thund'ring knell,
    And thine the light within me!   30

What man, in Fate's dark day of pow'r,
    While thoughts of thee upbore him,
Would shrink at danger's blackest lowr,
Or faint in life's last ebbing hour,
    If tears of thine fell o'er him?   35

But oh! if war's grim sweeping blast
    In vict'ry's radiance ended,
What Heav'n to find my [Jane] at last,
Within my arms to fold her fast,
    Our souls forever blended!   40

7

[NOW FARE THEE WELL OLD TWENTY-THREE!]

Now fare thee well old twenty-three!
No power, no art can thee retain
Eternity will roll away — Eternity!
And thou wilt *never* come again.

And welcome thou, young twenty-four,　　　　5
Thou bringer to men of joy and grief!
Whate'er thou bringest, in suffering sore
The patient heart in faith will hope relief.

8
[WHERE SHALL I FIND THEE]

Where shall I find thee, O sweet Peace!
Will the aimless tumult never cease?
Comes no respite, no release?
O where shall I find thee?

Could I reach thy soft still bower,   5
Ah! but for one little balmy hour,
And those Furies had no power
With fire-whips to lash me!

For my life is as a whirlwind blast,
Stormtost voyager I hurry past,   10
And on thousand rocks am cast:
Peace! Where shall I find thee?

Up Beyond that little Evening-star
Where the sheen speaks of thee from afar
Where my lost and loved ones are: 15
Peace! There shall I find thee?

For on Earth thou dwellest not, sweet Peace!
Here will din and discord never cease,
Comes no respite, no release:
Here shall I ne'er find thee!   20

9

TO JANE B. WELSH

So fare thee well, but not forever,
    My best, my loved, my only Jane!
What tho' in sadness we sever,
    Grieve not, we part to meet again.

Tho' storm and darkness lour above thee,   5
    Burns thro' it still one glad bright ray:
Think that in life and death I love thee,
    While wandering far my desert way!

Now one fond kiss, and then I leave thee,
    Not *yet* our strife with Fate is o'er!   10
Weep not, let not our parting grieve thee,
    Ere long we meet to part no more!

10
THUNDER-STORM [I]

The ploughman snores in weary length —
The oxen shade their ponderous strength —
The air is thick, and hot, and still,
And echo creeps from hill to hill.
Listless the scene, save where the hawk   5
In equipoise, keen scans the rock,
Intent for prey, or partridge springs,
Or trout, soft splashing, spreads its watery rings.
White clouds in distant silence rise,
And gradual reach a towering size,   10
Solid and deep — but soon the sky
With wider gloom arrests the eye —
The zenith low'rs, oppressed and hot
Hung heavy o'er the peasant's cot
In black suspense — now on the ear   15
Come distant rumblings; now more near,
More marked, more fearful; till the flash's glare
Dazzles the eye, and singes all the air —
A moment's pause — all safe — all sure —
But O! how breathlessly secure!   20
Heaven's concave groans,
And echo moans —
Another, brighter flash —
And then another peal,
That makes us feel   25
As if the vault were rent,
And heaven's artillery sent
Right over head, with deafening rattle,

Louder a thousand times than battle
In hot discharge; above, below,   30
One crackling, instant, overthrow.
Hark! on the crops
Come ponderous drops;
And now the awful dash,
And soaking, steeping splash —   35
The torrent roars,
The eagle soars;
The timid sheep
To shelter creep;
And all around   40
Seems dead and drowned,
While fainter rolls the solemn sound,
And paler lightnings pierce the ground.
Lo! all is o'er —
Bright as before   45
Peeps the blue azure forth,
And from the south, even to the north
A flood of radiance pours,
And drives the distant showers.
The welcome sun, with genial ray,   50
Dries the big rain-drop from the spray,
Sucks the clagged moisture from the bubbling earth,
And beams once more upon our buoyant mirth.

So comes misfortune, unforeseen,
To shade life's various, spangled scene,   55
Harrows our peace, and blasts the plans
Of such a chequered tale as man's;

Yet soon departs (small in extent
When measured by life's monument,)
And leaves the pleasure-favoured mind   60
To joys more tempered, more refined.

11
THUNDER STORM [II]

                             ————Now deep
Nature had sunk in darkness and in sleep —
The dawn yet peeped not — stillness reigned intense,
(Far, far more terrible than turbulence,)
Save where the rustling leaf, the beetle's drone,   5
The bat's, the night-hawk's shriek, or noise unknown,
Or the owl's hoot, long echoing far and near,
Fearfully solemn met the vacant ear.
Sultry and clogged the air, an aching load
Hung o'er the traveller's brow — the dusky road   10
Soon merged in blackness, as th' impending sky
In pitchy horror pained the baffled eye.
He mends his pace, in palpitating haste
To gain his home — Alas! his toil how waste,
With lightning striving — swift it fires the air,   15
Darting its forky terrors with a glare
So white, so instant, through the solid black,
That the scared soul seeks shelter in the crack
Of bursting thunder — every following flash
Lights more terrific the black forest's crash.   20
Hark to the shattered oak! behold it, low,
In severed ruin bow,
Then blaze aloft — on right — on left —
Another, then another cleft —
And shall *he* then escape?   25
Saw you yon lightning leap
In pronged divergence to the furrowed ground?
There shall his corpse be found.

Instant his fate!
Such may await   30
We know not whom, nor when, nor where,
And, through the turmoiled air,
To the horizon's utmost verge,
Dull thunder *rumbles* out his funeral dirge.
With aching brow,   35
In listening sorrow,
His widow now
Shall wait the morrow.
The morrow brings him not — he lies
Where the hot lightning sealed his eyes.   40
But busy bruit, mischievously kind,
Will hint her loss, and strive to sooth her mind,
And, after torturing suspense, will try
To introduce her to her misery.

12
THE SOWER'S SONG

Now hands to seedsheet, boys,
We step and we cast; old Time's on wing;
And would ye partake of Harvest's joys,
The corn must be sown in Spring.
　　Fall gently and still, good corn,　　　　　　5
　　Lie warm in thy earthy bed;
　　And stand so yellow some morn,
　　For beast and man must be fed.

Old Earth is a pleasure to see
In sunshiny cloak of red and green;　　　　　　10
The furrow lies fresh; this Year will be
As Years that are past have been.
　　Fall gently, &c.

Old Mother, receive this corn,
The son of Six Thousand golden sires:　　　　　15
All these on thy kindly breast were born;
One more thy poor child rquires.
　　Fall gently, &c.

Now steady and sure again,
And measure of stroke and step we keep;　　　　20
Thus up and thus down we cast our grain:
Sow well, and you gladly reap.
　　Fall gently and still, good corn,
　　Lie warm in thy earthy bed;
　　And stand so yellow some morn,　　　　　　25
　　For beast and man must be fed.

13
CUI BONO

What is Hope? A smiling rainbow
    Children follow through the wet;
'Tis not here, still yonder, yonder:
    Never urchin found it yet.

What is Life? A thawing iceboard   5
    On a sea with sunny shore; —
Gay we sail; it melts beneath us;
    We are sunk, and seen no more.

What is Man? A foolish baby,
    Vainly strives, and fights, and frets;   10
Demanding all, deserving nothing; —
    One small grave is what he gets.

14
[THE HILDEBRANDS]

The Hildebrands, the Philips and the Borgias
Where are they now? Behind the scene; mute as
The millions whom they butchered in their rage.
Hard task they had, poor men: what was their wage?
From God, we know not, but may dread the worst;   5
From man, a grave and memory forever curst:
Who worships self a foolish thought has ween'd,
Must offer *all,* and find his God — a Fiend.

15
[SCOTLAND PRIDES]

Scotland prides her in the "Bonnet Blue,"
That it brooks no stain in Love or War:
Be it, on Ottilie's head, a token true
Of my Scottish Love to kind Weimar!

16
[TO THE POET]

For th' Heaven-gifted still an earthly Gift have I!
Some kingly robe, belike? Some jewel priceless-fair?
A Gift no King's or Croesus' yellow heaps could buy:
True love from Woman's heart, this tress of Woman's hair!

17

MY OWN FOUR WALLS

The storm and night are on the waste,
Wild thro' the wind the herdsman calls,
As fast, on willing Nag, I haste,
      Home to my own four walls.

Black, tossing clouds, with scarce a glimmer,   5
Envelope Earth, like sevenfold palls:
But wifekin watches, coffee-pot doth simmer,
      Home in my own four walls!

A home and wife I too have got,
A hearth to blaze whate'er befal[l] s!   10
What needs a man that I have not
      Within my own four walls?

King George has palaces of pride,
And armed grooms must ward their halls:
With one stout bolt, I safe abide   15
      Within my own four walls.

Not all his men may sever this,
It yields to Friend's, not Monarch's calls,
My whinstone house my Castle is,
      I have my own four walls.   20

When fools or Knaves do make a rout,
With gigman dinners, balls, cabals,
I turn my back, and shut them out;
      These are my own four walls.

The moorland house, tho' rude it be,   25
May stand the brunt, when prouder falls;
'Twill screen my wife, my Books and me,
        All in my own four walls.

18
THE SIGH

O sigh not so, my fond and faithful Wife,
In sad remembrance, or in boding fear:
This is not Life, this phantasm Type of Life,
What is there to rejoice or mourn for here?

Be it, no wealth, nor fame, nor post is ours,   5
Small Blessedness for infinite Desire:
But has the King his wish in Windsor's Towers?
Or but the common lot: "meat, clothes, and fire"?

Lone stands our Home amid the sullen moor,
Its threshold by few friendly feet betrod;   10
Yet *we* are here, we Two, still true, tho' poor,
And this too is THE WORLD — the "City of God"!

O'erhangs us not th' Infinitude of Sky,
Where all the starry Lights revolve and shine?
Does not that Universe within us lie,   15
And move, — its maker, or itself divine?

And we, my Love, life's waking Dream once done
Shall sleep (to wondrous Lands) on other's breast,
And all we loved and toiled for, one by one,
Shall join us there, and wearied be at rest!   20

Then sigh not so, my fond and faithful Wife,
But striving well, have hope, be of good cheer;
Not Rest but worthy Labour is the soul of Life;
Not that, but this, is to be look'd and wish'd for here.

19
[O TIME]

O Time, how thou fliest,
False heart, how thou liest;
Leave chattering and fretting,
Betake thee to doing and getting!

20
[THY QUIET GOODNESS]

Thy quiet goodness, spirit pure and brave
What boots it now with tears to tell?
The path to Rest lies thro' the Grave:
Loved Sister, take our long Farewell!

21
THE WANDERING SPIRITS

1

Hail, pilgrim! In Space's Infinitude,
In Eternity's quick-passing moment;
Here strangely our paths meet together:
    Whence comes the wayfarer and who?

2

From far of a truth was my journeying: 5
From bourne of this thousand-sunn'd All,
Began when first Time was created!

1

'Tis far, as thou sayest, yet near us,
The Bosom of God.

2

    Whence I come? From the Depths   10
Of Being's inscrutable Ocean, that onward
Of Light and of Darkness, of Birth and of Death, —
Still floweth in Passion and Action, —
From Myst'ry to Myst'ry: the whirl of that
Chaos awoke me; and here for a space   15
I have Figure: I Am, and Appear.

1

Thy errand, strange Spirit?

2

Who knows it?
To wander! To wander!

1

Sore marrd is thy face,   20
In those glances, so restless, so wearied,
Stern anger oft glow'd, and the gentler
Effulgence of tears?

2

Lo! these Garments of Flesh
I wear; and still onwards and onwards   25
A voice doth command me, and Pleasure
I tasted and Pain, and Love also and Hate, —
Am compassd with Storms and with Radiance —
Sleep too is vouchsafed me; but nowhere is Rest.

1

Ha Pilgrim no Spirit art thou but a Man!   30
Embrace me my Brother! we two are as Exiles
Beneath the lone sky, ah and far from our Homeland
Let each on the lov'd heart find solace and strength.

2

Embrace, and farewell!

1

Must we forth, and alone?   35

2

To Darkness, and Silence, and Death!

1

Yet with God
For Guidance?

2

Yea, God.

1

And who knows   40
But (the Darkness a veil) in that Silence is Light
And the Rest which thou seekest?

2

As HE shall have willed!

1

And the Parted may meet?

2

As HE wills!   45
Both. We are far and yet near: fare thee well!

22
THE BEETLE

Poor hobbling Beetle, needst not haste;
Should Traveller Traveller thus alarm?
Pursue thy journey through the waste,
Not foot of mine shall work thee harm.

Who knows what errand grave thou   hast,   5
'Small family' — that have not dined?
Lodged under pebble, there they fast,
Till head of house have raised the wind!

Man's bread lies 'mong the feet of men;
For cark and moil sufficient cause!   10
Who cannot sow would reap; — and then
In Beetledom are no Poor-Laws.

And if thy Wife and thou agree
But ill, as like when short of victual,
I swear, the Public Sympathy   15
Thy fortune meriteth, poor Beetle.

Alas, and I should do thee skaith,
To realms of Night with heeltap send!
Who judg'd thee worthy pains of Death? —
On Earth, save me, without a Friend!   20

Pass on, poor Beetle, venerable
Art thou, were wonders ne'er so rife;

Thou hast what Bel to Tower of Babel
Not gave: the chief of wonders —LIFE.

Also of 'ancient family,'   25
Though small in size, of feature dark!
What Debrett's Peer surpasseth thee?
Thy Ancestor was in Noah's Ark.

23
ABSENT

Far in desart's depths, what Rose is flowering!
    Wherefore droops that Rose today?
'Tis her "Sun" is hid, so clouds are lowering:
    Love! thy Lover's far away!

For she's mine, my own, that Rose of Roses,   5
    And my cheek her leaves do kiss,
All its Heaven-perfume her heart uncloses:
    Can a mortal taste such bliss!

Roses few, and ever with pruning, weeding,
    Wealth or Pomp or Power will yield;   10
But the fairest Rose of God's own Eden
    Blooms in my poor rocky field!

O thou Heart's-Rose, droop not, cease thy pining!
    Long forsaken canst thou be?
Bright tomorrow morn thy Sun is shining;   15
    Over the hills, I haste to thee.

What for me were Earth, or what were Heaven?
    And my own lov'd one not there?
Might a life, a death with her, be given,
    Fate! I had no other prayer.   20

24
[FOR THE POET]

All mute and dim as Shadows gray,
His Scottish Friends the Friend descries:
Let Love evoke them into day,
To questions a kind shape kind replies.

25
[PRIEST—RIDDEN]

Priest-ridden, wife-ridden, plague-ridden,
    Who escapes his lot?
Bearing, forbearing, paying, obeying,
    Will ye, will ye not.
Child-ridden, tremble at my Doll's pouting: 5
    Fortune, spare me that!

26
[OH! LIFE TURMOIL]

Oh! life turmoil — to-day — to-morrow
    Unfathomed thing thou wert and art:
In sight, in blindness, joy and sorrow
    The wondrous Thomas plays his part.

Awhile behold him flesh-clothed *spirit,*
    He reaps and sows the allotted hours,
Would much bequeath, did much inherit,
    Oh! help the helpless, heavenly powers.

27
DRUMWHIRN BRIDGE
OVER THE RIVER ORR. — BUILT, 1832

Meek autumn midnight glancing,
   The stars above hold sway,
I bend, in muse advancing,
   To lonesome Orr my way.

Its rush in drowsy even 5
   Can make the waste less dead:
Short pause beneath void Heaven,
   Then back again to bed!

Hoho! 'mong deserts moory,
   See here the craftsman's hand; 10
Vain now, bleak Orr, thy fury,
   On whinstone arch I stand.

Dull Orr, thou moorland river
   By man's eye rarely seen,
Thou gushest on for ever, 15
   And wert while earth has been.

There o'er thy crags and gravel,
   Thou sing'st an unknown song,
In tongue no clerks unravel!
   Thou'st sung it long and long 20

From Being's Source it bounded,
   The morn when time began;
Since thro' this moor has sounded,
   Unheard or heard of man.

That day they crossed the Jordan,   25
    When Hebrew trumpets rang,
Thy wave no foot was fording,
    Yet here in moor it sang.

And I, while thou's meandered,
    Was not, have come to be,   30
Apart so long have wandered,
    This moment meet with thee.

Old Orr, thou mystic water!
    No Ganges holier is;
That was Creation's daughter;   35
    What was it fashioned *this*?

The whinstone Bridge is builded,
    Will hang a hundred year;
When bridge to time has yielded,
    The brook will still be here.   40

Farewell, poor moorland river:
    We parted and we met;
Thy journeyings are for ever,
    Mine art not ended yet.

28

CRICHOPE LINN
Loquitur Genius Loci:

Cloister'd vault of living rocks,
Here have I my darksome dwelling;
Working sing to stones and stocks,
Where, beneath, my waves go welling.

Beams flood-borne athwart me cast,   5
Arches, see, and aisles moist-gleaming!
Sounds for ay my organ-blast:
Grim Cathedral shaped in Dreaming!

Once a Lake, and next a Linn,
Still my Course sinks deeper boring;   10
Cleft far up, where light steals in,
That as "Gullet" once was roaring.

For three thousand years or more,
Savage I, none praised or blamed me: —
Maiden's hand unbolts my Door;   15
Look of Loveliness hath tamed me.

Maiden mild! This levell'd Path
Emblem is of her bright being;
Long thro' Discord, Darkness, Scath,
Goes she helping, ruling, freeing.   20

Thank her, Wand'rer, as thou now
Gazest safe thro' gloom so dreary:

Rough things plain make likewise thou,
And of well-doing be not weary.

"Gullet" one day Cleft shall be,   25
Crichope Cave have new sunk-story;
Thousand years away shall flee:
Flees not Goodness or its glory.

29
AN HANNCHEN,

Meine "WERKE", allzu lümp'gen Kinder
  Harten Schicksals, des verhackten Sinn,
Stehn zur Rede, Dir, wie armen Sünder,
  Liebste nicht zu strenge Richterinn!

30
ADIEU

Let time and chance combine, combine,
Let time and chance combine;
The fairest love from heaven above,
That love of yours was mine,
     My dear,   5
That love of yours was mine.

The past is fled and gone, and gone,
The past is fled and gone;
If nought but pain to me remain,
I'll fare in memory on,   10
     My dear,
I'll fare in memory on.

The saddest tears must fall, must fall,
The saddest tears must fall;
In weal or woe, in this world below, 15
I love you ever and all,
     My dear,
I love you ever and all.

A long road full of pain, of pain,
A long road full of pain;   20
One soul, one heart, sworn ne'er to part, —
We ne'er can meet again,
     My dear,
We ne'er can meet again.

Hard fate will not allow, allow,   25
Hard fate will not allow;
We blessed were as the angels are, —
Adieu forever now,
                    My dear,
Adieu forever now.

31
TO-DAY

So here hath been dawning
Another blue Day:
Think wilt thou let it
Slip useless away.

Out of Eternity   5
This new Day is born;
Into Eternity,
At night, will return.

Behold it aforetime
No eye ever did: 10
So soon it forever
From all eyes is hid.

Here hath been dawning
Another blue Day:
Think wilt thou let it   15
Slip useless away.

32
FORTUNA

The wind blows east, the wind blows west,
And the frost falls and the rain:
A weary heart went thankful to rest,
And must rise to toil again, 'gain,
And must rise to toil again.   5

The wind blows east, the wind blows west,
And there comes good luck and bad;
The thriftiest man is the cheerfullest;
'Tis a thriftless thing to be sad, sad,
'Tis a thriftless thing to be sad.   10

The wind blows east, the wind blows west;
Ye shall know a tree by its fruit:
This world, they say, is worst to the best; —
But a dastard has evil to boot, boot,
But a dastard has evil to boot.   15

The wind blows east, the wind blows west;
What skills it to mourn or to talk?
A journey I have, and far ere I rest;
I must bundle my wallets and walk, walk,
I must bundle my wallets and walk.   20

The wind does blow as it lists alway;
Canst thou change this world to thy mind?
The world will wander its own wise way;
I also will wander mine, mine,
I also will wander mine.   25

33
TO A SWALLOW BUILDING UNDER OUR EAVES

Thou too hast travelled, little fluttering thing,
Hast seen the world, and now thy weary wing
    Thou too must rest.
But much, my little Bird, couldst thou but tell,
I'd give to know why here thou lik'st so well   5
    To build thy nest.

For thou hast passed fair places in thy flight;
A world lay all beneath thee where to light;
    And strange thy taste!
Of all the varied scenes that met thine eye,   10
Of all the spots for building 'neath the sky,
    To choose this waste!

Did Fortune try thee? was thy little purse
Perchance run low, and thou afraid of worse
    Felt here secure?   15
Ah no! thou need'st not gold, thou happy one!
Thou know'st it not! Of all God's creatures, man
    Alone is poor!

What was it then? Some mystic turn of thought,
Caught under German eaves, and hither brought,   20
    Marring thine eye
For the world's loveliness, till thou art grown
A sober thing that dost but mope and moan,
    Not knowing why?

Nay, if thy mind be sound, I need not ask,   25
Since here I see thee *working* at the *task,*
   With wing and beak.
A well-laid scheme doth that small head contain,
At which thou work'st, brave Bird, with might and main,
   Nor more need'st seek!   30

In truth, I rather take it thou hast got,
By instinct wise, much sense about thy lot,
   And hast small care
Whether an Eden or a Desert be
Thy home; so thou remain'st alive, and free   35
   To skim the air!

God speed thee, pretty Bird! May thy small nest
With little ones all in good time be blest!
   I love thee much!
For well thou managest that life of thine,   40
While I! — O ask not what I do with mine!
   Would it were such!

34
[THIRTY-NINE ENGLISH ARTICLES]

Thirty-nine English Articles,
Ye wondrous little particles,
Did God shape his Universe really by *you*?
In that case, I swear it,
And solemnly declare it,   5
This logic of M[orri]s's is true.

35
SONG I
[MR THOMAS CAMPBELL]

Mr Thomas Campbell,
Prickly as a bramble,
Sang of the Pleasures of Hope;
Men gave him a pension,
Of his glory made mention: —   5
Now out on the ramble
Without scheme or intention,
Drink brandy, and sulkily mope!

36
SONG II
[FRANCIS LORD JEFFREY]

Francis Lord Jeffrey,
Thou man of great fame,
Reviewer most peppery,
Shadow of a name!

What good can it do thee   5
That dolts should exclaim,
In their pilgriming to thee,
"O man of great fame!"

All fame is a shadow,
Great or small much the same,   10
What use of it have you or had you
O man of great fame?

The bright Blue and Yellow
Rather dim it became;
A small cheery fellow   15
Once man of great fame.

37
SONG III
[POOR THOMAS CAIREL]

Poor Thomas *Cairel,*
Foolishest of men,
Bought him new apparel;
And what followed then?

Bought him new apparel,   5
Lectured unto men,
Gaped and gasped, poor Cairel,
Foolishest of men.

He wrote a Revolution,
Book without its like;   10
Then he took a resolution
That he was a wretched tike.

Sartor called *Resartus*
This they published thence;
"May no chance e'er part us!"   15
Nonsense said to Sense.

But then came no money,
Not a coin of money in,
Then was gall instead of honey,
'Stead of peace was din.   20

Hapless Thomas Cairel
Foolishest of men
Bought him new apparel
And what followed then?

38
[COCK-A-DOODLE-DOO]

Cock-a-doodle-doo, cuck, cuck,
    What an ass in Carlyle,
Stood not, on our guide-post stuck,
    The invaluable Sterling!

Cock-a-doodle-doo, this, this,   5
    This the road, ye dolts you!
Road to Nowhere not amiss,
    Road to Somewhere jolts so!

39
[THE LASSES OF THE CANONGATE]

The lasses of the Canongate
[M] ay kaim their yellow hair
But Leslie's bonny men I trow
[R] eturn to them nae mair.

O bonny are your looks, my dears   5
And bright your bonny e'en
But hame come not the lads the night
That marched away yestreen.

They gaed by Colrunspath to fight
An army brave and fair   10
But Crommel wi' the foul friends' help
Has blawn them to the air.

Has blawn them to the air, my dears
Has skailed them wide and far.
O wae light on't that Scottish men   15
Should tine the art of war!

And many a blooming face last night
Is pale and cauld the day
Their broken arms bestrew the ground
They're slain or fled away.   20

For lovers' hands the horses' hoofs
Caress those faces dear:
In gory mud, our bonny men,
Thurst down by sword and spear!

The lasses of the Canongate &c &c —— nae mair - (!) -   25

40
[GAE 'WA WI]

Gae 'wa wi your kistfu whistles my man
   Gae to the bound road and awa
Your service-books, gowns and soubristles my man
   We canna do wi them ava.

41
[THE BUILDER OF THIS UNIVERSE]

The Builder of this Universe was wise,
He plann'd all souls, all systems, planets, particles:
The Plan He shap'd all Worlds and Æons by,
Was — Heavens! — Was thy small Nine-and-thirty Articles?

42
[UNUSED TO TRADE]

Unused to trade, and sore afraid
Lest I mistaken be,
I take the Purse, for better or worse,
And yield it, Dear, to thee!

Autograph Poems and Questionable Attributions

for Thomas Carlyle

1
[LITTLE DID MY MOTHER THINK]

Little did my mother think
    That day she cradled me,
What land I was to travel in,
    Or what death I should dee,
        Oh, foolish thee.   5

2
[O BUSK YE]

'For there's seven foresters in yon forest;
    And them I want to see, see,
And them I want to *see* (and shoot down)!

3
[WHAT IS HEAVEN?]

What is Heaven? and what are ye
Who its brief expanse inherit?
What are suns and spheres which flee
With the instinct of that spirit
    Of which ye are but a part?   5
    Drops which nature's mighty heart
    Drives thro' thinnest veins —
What is Heaven? a globe of dew,
Filling in the morning new
        Some eyed flower who see young leaves waken   10
On an unimagined world:
        Constellated suns unshaken,
Orbits measureless, are furled
        In that frail and faded sphere
        With ten millions gathered there,   15
        To tremble, gleam, and disappear.

4
DIRGE: "FEAR NO MORE"

Fear no more the heat o' the sun,
Nor the furious winter's rages;
Thou thy weary task hast done,
Home art gone, and ta'en thy wages.

Hurts thee now no harsh behest,   5
Toil or shame or sin or danger;
Trouble's storm has got to rest,
To his place the wayworn Stranger.

Want is done, and grief and pain,
Done is all thy bitter weeping;   10
Thou art safe from wind and rain,
In thy Mother's bosom sleeping.

Fear no more the heat o' th' sun,
Nor the furious winter's rages;
Thou thy weary task hast done,   15
Home art gone, and ta'en thy wages.

5
[SIMON BRODIE]

Simon Brodie had a cow;
He Lost his cow, and he could na find her:
When he had done what man could do,
The cow cam hame and her tail behind her.

6
[EINSAM, EINSAM]

Einsam, einsam, das bin ich nicht
Denn die Geister meiner Geliebten,
Entfernten und Todten,
Sie umgeben mich.

7
ILIAS (AMERICANA) IN NUCE

Peter *of the North* (*to* Paul *of the South*). "Paul, you
unaccountable scoundrel, I find you hire your servants for
life, not by the month or year as I do! You are going
straight to Hell, you ----!"

Paul. "Good words, Peter! The risk is my own; I am   5
willing to take the risk. Hire you your servants by the
month or the day, and get straight to Heaven; leave me
to my own method."

Peter. "No, I won't. I will beat your brains out first!"
(*And is trying dreadfully ever since, but cannot yet manage*   10
it.)

8
[WANDERING IN A STRANGE LAND]

Though wandering in a strange land
Though in the waste no altar stand
Take comfort, thou art not alone
While Faith hath marked thee for her own.

Wouldst thou a Temple? look above   5
The heavens stretch over thee in Love:
A Book! For thine Evangile scan
The wondrous history of man.

The holy band of saints renowned
Embrace thee brotherlike around   10
Then sufferings and their triumphs rise
In hymns immortal to the skies.

What though no organ-peal be heard?
In harmony the winds are stirred
And there the morning stars upraise   15
Their ancient songs of deathless praise.

9
[THERE WAS A PIPER HAD A COO]

There was a Piper had a Coo,
And he had nocht to give her;
He took his pipes and play'd a spring,
And bade the Coo consider;
The Coo consider'd wi' hersel',   5
That mirth wad ne'er fill her;
'Gie me a pickle ait strae,
And sell your wind for siller!'

Translations of Thomas Carlyle

1
THE FISHER
Variations by Hypercriticus Minimus

The water rush'd the water swell'd;
    A Fisher floating there
Calm gaz'd upon the hooks he held;
    Felt little joy or care.

Cool to the heart, no heed he gave   5
    But to his flick'ring lines;
When lo! uprising from the wave
    A beauteous mermaid shines.

She softly spoke, she softly sang,
    "Ah cruel! wherefore wish   10
With wit of man and wiles of man
    To lure my harmless fish?

Coudst thou but know how merry plays
    The Minnow down below,
Thou'dst haste with me where pleasure stays   15
    To hide from toil and woe.

Bends not the Moon to dip, — the Sun
    Wave-gilding, in the Main?
And doubly bright their race to run
    Return they not again?   20

Does Heaven's vast dome not lure thee
    Here glass'd in lucid blue?

Does not thy face here shadow'd lure th[ee]
    Down to eternal dew?"

The water rush'd, the water swell'd,   25
    It lav'd his naked foot;
His heart with fond desire was fill'd
    As at love's soft salute.

She sang, she charm'd tho' awing h[im]
    More wild his bosom burn'd;   30
Half leaning — she half drawing him
    He sank and ne'er return'd.

2
FAUST'S CURSE

If thro' th' abyss of terror stealing
Those touching sounds my purpose stay'd
Some ling'ring trace of childish feeling
With voice of merrier times betray'd;
I curse the more whate'er environs   5
The cheated soul with juggling shows,
Those hearts' allurements, fancy's syrens
That bind us to this den of woes.
Accursed first the tinsel dreaming
Of innate worth our spirits weave!   10
Each hollow form so lovely seeming
That shines our senses to deceive!
A curse on all one seed that scatters
Of hopes our name from Death to save!
On all *as ours* on Earth that flatters   15
As child or wife, as plough or slave!
A curse on mammon when with treasures
He tempts to high and hardy deeds,
When spreading soft the couch of pleasures
The drousy soul he captive leads!   20
A curse on juice of grapes deceiving,
On Love's wild thrill, of raptures first!
A curse on hoping, on believing!
And patience more than all be curs'd!

3
[WHO NEVER ATE HIS BREAD IN SORROW]

Who never ate his bread in sorrow,
    Who never spent the darksome hours
Weeping, and watching for the morrow,
    He knows ye not, ye gloomy Powers.

To earth, this weary earth, ye bring us,   5
    To guilt ye let us heedless go,
Then leave repentance fierce to wring us:
    A moment's guilt, an age of woe!

4

CONFESSIO FIDEI

I mean to be quite easy and gay,
To see something new on each [new] day,
To the moment merrily trusting,
No thought on the past or the future casting.
So, look, to the Kaiser I sold my bacon   5
And by him let the charge of all needful be taken
Order me on to the whistling cannon shot
Over the red and roaring Rhine,
The second man must go to pot, —
I mount and ride without loss of time.   10
But farther I humbly beg and pray,
That in other things I may have my way.
Marketenderin
Cousin! since then I've been wide and far,
To-day we come, to-morrow we go,
As it happens the besom of war   15
Shakes one and sweeps one to and fro
Wallenstein
Our life was but a battle and a march,
And like the wind's blast, never-resting, homeless,
We stormed across the war-convulsed earth.
Kürassier —
This sword of ours is no plough or spade   20
You cannot delve or reap with the iron blade;
For us there springs no seed, no cornfield grows
The soldier no home nor kindred knows,
Must wander over the face of the earth,
Must warm his hands at another's hearth,   25

To the pomp of towns he bids adieu,
In the village green with its cheerful game,
In the vintage [time] or harvest-home,
No part or lot can the soldier claim.
Tell me then what good or worth he has   30
If the soldier cease to honour himself?
Leave him nothing of his own, what wonder
The creature should burn and kill and plunder?

5

[WHERE LEMON-TREES DO BLOOM]

Know'st thou the land where lemon-trees do bloom,
And oranges like gold in leafy gloom;
A gentle wind from deep blue heaven blows,
The mystle thick, and high the laurel grows?
Know'st thou it, then?   5
     'Tis there! 'tis there,
O my belov'd one, I with thee would go!

Know'st thou the house, its porch with pillars tall?
The rooms do glitter, glitters bright the hall,
And marble statues stand, and look me on: 10
What's this, poor child, to thee they've done?
Know'st thou it, then?
     'Tis there! 'tis there,
O my protector, I with thee would go!

Know'st thou the mountain, bridge that hangs on cloud? 15
The mules in mist grope o'er the torrent loud,
In caves lie coil'd the dragon's ancient brood,
The crag leaps down and over it the flood:
Know'st thou it, then?
     'Tis there! 'tis there,   20
Our way runs; O my father, wilt thou go?

6
THE VILLAGE

What village dare
with mine compare?
Its hillocks green,
And meads between;
None else I meet   5
Are half so sweet —
A scene so rich,
Well might be witch
A Dietrich's taste —   10
Its rocks, how vast!
Its waving grains,
And grassy plains,
And forests blue,
To close the view!   15
Flocks calmly crop
Each sunny slope,
While I look down
Upon my own,
My lov'd retreat   20
Contentment's seat,
Where elm and vine,
Thick intertwine;
And all the day,
A hermit gay,   25
In vernal ease,
I catch the breeze.

Green garlands sweep
The craggy steep,

The poplar fair,   30
Shakes in blue air,
The limpid brook,
Now, in the nook,
With pebbled purl,
And eddying curl,   35
Would fain elude,
In coyest mood,
'Mong leafy sprays,
The wanderer's gaze;
Now, in its face,   40
Faithful pourtrays,
Hills, flocks, and trees,
With nature's ease;
While its still wave,
Fish smoothly cleave,   45
And sink and rise
In pictured skies.

Fair is the scene;
But yet, I wean,
Eliza's eyes   50
Are Paradise!
With rising sun,
Our joy begun,
Light robed and fair
She hies her there,   55
Where morning's Queen
The flowery green
With tears bedews,
Bright gleams diffuse,

From each wet blade, 60
With pearls down-weighed —
Buds open spread:
Each flower's head,
Glories to rise
In gorgeous dyes — 65
Yet — of all there,
She the most fair.

Now the sun high
Rides in the sky;
And in the pool, 70
I long to cool
My tired limbs, —
Where the brook skims,
Wooing the rock,
Sheltered I walk, 75
And take the path,
Which to the bath
Of shepherds leads;
And I must needs
This freshening take, 80
Calm as a lake,
The gelid stream
'Mid noon-day's steam.
So circles round
Joy without bound; 85
Nor need I fly,
Satiety.

O happiness!
Were the risk less

Of marrings rude;   90
Could my fresh blood
Thy living charm
For ever warm,
Then should delight,
Lavished, alight   95
On all mankind —
I would unbind
Each jealous tie,
And, soaring high,
Attune my lays   100
To pleasure's praise.
But this were vain —
For what than pain
On earth more sure!
What less secure   105
Than sensual joy!
Why then employ
Our being so
On casual show!
Pleasures decoy   110
But to destroy —
A higher hope
Must point the scope
Of man's emprize,
Who, when he dies,   115
Enters, in strife,
And endless life,
Where but one name,
Can found his claim —

One temper here,   120
Meeter to bear
The dazzling holiness
Of Heaven.

7
[ENWERI TELLS US]

Enweri tells us, a most royal man,
The deepest heart and highest head to scan:
"In every place, at every time, thy surest chance
Lies in Decision, Justice, Tolerance."

8
[FOR THE TIE IS SNAPT ASUNDER]

For the tie is snapt asunder,
    Trust and loving hope are fled;
Can I tell, in fear and wonder,
    With what dangers now bested,
I, cut off from friend and brother,   5
    Like the widow in her woe,
With the one and not the other,
    On and on, my way must go!

9

[DARK CHAIN]

Wilt thou, at thy mirror smiling, place
On a neck so light so grave a toy,
Think that nought so well the wife can grace
As when wedded wife brings husband joy.

10
THE OSCULATION OF THE STARS

Wide asunder in the azure All,
Mayst thou see two Starlets moving
That from far, so gladly, yet so sadly,
For a thousand years, were looking, loving;
Till a brief ambrosial kiss,   5
One, but one, as fast they rush together,
Brings them love's ethereal bliss,
And again, thro' pathless Space they sever:
Yet will Love, god-consecrate,
Flame for ever thro' the Night of Fate.   10

Late it was the time had come
When those Starlets two united,
And, amid the dancing and the glancing
Of remotest Suns, did kiss delighted;
Lo! when least for her I look,   15
Cometh she I aye shall love so kindly,
One fond Kiss she gave and took.
And stern hap did part us blindly:
Yet will Love, god-consecrate,
Flame for ever thro' the Night of Fate.   20

11
[MASON-LODGE]

The Mason's ways are
A type of Existence,
And his persistence
Is as the days are
Of men in this world.   5

The Future hides in it
Gladness and sorrow;
We press still throw,
Nought that abides in it
Daunting us, — onward.   10

And solemn before us,
Veiled, the dark Portal,
Goal of all mortal: —
Stars silent rest o'er us,
Graves under us silent!   15

While earnest thou gazest,
Comes boding of terror,
Comes phantasm and error,
Perplexes the bravest
With doubt and misgiving.   20

But heard are the Voices, —
Heard are the Sages,
The Worlds and the Ages:
'Choose well; your choice is
Brief and yet endless: 25

Here eyes do regard you,
In Eternity's stillness;
Here is all fulness,
Ye brave, to reward you;
Work, and despair not.'   30

12
THE NIGHTINGALE

The nightingale had flown her ways,
The Spring allures her back: —
Of new she has not learned anything,
Sings her dear old songs again.

The Poems of Jane Welsh Carlyle

Haddington, 20th July, 182[4]

1

THE RIVAL BROTHERS:
FRAGMENT OF A PLAY BY JANE BAILLIE WELSH

The Rival Brothers

A Tragedy

In 5 acts by Jane Baillie Welsh
Aged 14

Dramatis Personae
Men

Lord Clarence ⎫
D'Auville ⎪
De Courcy ⎪   Women
Mortimer ⎬   Adelaide
Horatio   ⎪   Servants &c
Stanmore ⎪
Oreztan   ⎭

Act I. Scene I. An Inn.
Enter Lord Clarence & D'Auville

D'Auville
My Lord, indulge not unavailing grief;
All may be well; thy son may yet exist,
And years of happiness to come
Reward thee for thy many sorrows past —

L.C. Oh! Tell not me of happiness!
          My ears are unaccustomed to the sound
          I once indeed possessed the heavenly gift;
          But Oh: twas but to feel its loss more great
          Its very shadow has deserted me
          D'Auville thou hast never yet fully learned   1
          The fatal causes of thy friend's distress;
          And tho' the sad recital gives me pain,
          'Twill ease my heart to share its griefs with thee

D.A. Would you could give me all,
          For you too long have borne the heavy load;
          Despair, too long, has sat upon thy brow;
          Too long has chid the least approach of hope —

L.C. When you have heard my wretched story
          You will judge how much I've cause to mourn —
          The lovely Julia first enslaved my heart,   20
          The Daughter of a Nobleman of Lisbon.
          Her noble race, and wealth, tho' powerful
          Appeared to me, as far beneath herself
          As tapers burning in the brilliant day;
          I loved, And (Oh. transporting thought)
          I was beloved —
          Her father kindly gave her to my arms:
          Oh! I shall ne'er forget the blissful hour
          That joined our hands and made the Angel mine —
          A rapid year passed on in perfect bliss;   30
          Then heaven gave an Infant to my arms;
          Each youthful grace adorned the lovely boy;
          Forgive a father's fondness —

D'A. Go on my Lord, I long to hear,
    What unforeseen event,
    Could cause so great a change —

L.C. Another year rolled on
    Blessed as the former,
    And then, another son, his mother's image,
    Clung to my happy heart —   40
    I heard at length, the tidings of my father's death;
    I wished to visit once again my native realm —
    Julia, and my Theodore embarked
    In the first vessel, which for England sailed;
    Oh fatal rashness, why did we ever part?
    For then at least we might have died together
    Britain they ne'er were destined to behold
    The ship was lost amidst the merciless waves
    And in the Ocean all my hopes were sunk —

D'A. Say not all my Lord,   50
    You had yet one comfort left

L.C. My son, you mean? —
    Oh! no.
    My Frederick too was severed from my arms;
    With him, I mournfully embarked;
    Almost wishing that another storm
    Would, Once again unite me to my Julia —
    Another lot, fate had decreed for us;
    Our ship became the Conquest of the Moors,
    And we Ourselves their slaves: —   60
    The monsters deaf to all a father's prayers

Tore the helpless infant from my arms;
Nor have I ever since beheld my Boy;
Ten dismal years of slavery rolled on —
At length a country man,
Enslaved as well as I, escaped,
And with a generosity scarce ever found
But in a Briton's soul,
Obtained my ransom —
For six years more I vainly sought my child   70
And now, heart-broken, childless, in despair,
I have returned to die among my friends —

D'A. Since you have dismissed all earthly hope,
Yet there is consolation;
No guilt of yours hath caused your sufferings,
And Heaven will in joy drown the despair,
Which it has doomed to be on earth they share —

                                        Exeunt

Scene II
An Apartment in the Castle

Adelaide alone (weeping)
Oh! cruel, cruel fortune

                                enter Mortimer
Mort: My Life, My Adelaide, what mean these tears:
       Oh! Tell me quickly nor refuse your Mortimer
       The privilege of love — to share thy sorrows

Adel: Who would not weep?

Oh! Mortimer the cloud which long has hung
Suspended o'er our love
At length has burst
And the dark storm of woe
Falls thick on every side.   10

Mort: Alas! what means my Love?

Adel: Fain would my tongue deny its office,
      And refuse to wound thy gentle breast;
      But sorrow, bursting from my painful heart;
      Compels my voice to give it utterance —
      Yes, Mortimer,
      Stern duty bids us part,
      And Adelaide must obey.

Mort—Just Heavens! My fears then were not groundless
      I long have marked the partial eye   20
      With which your father views your youthful stranger,
      And he has destined him (distraction's in the thought)
      For Adelaide's Husband;
      Is it not so?

Adel: It is but too true —

Mort: This is a blow indeed:
      Support me Heaven or I sink beneath it —

Adel—Mortimer hear me —
      Ever since my Sainted mother's death,
      My father's comfort has been placed in me,   30

And shall I now with disobedience,
Reward his tender cares, his anxious love,
And blast at once his fondest hopes;
Oh! no! it must not be:
Yet if you look so very very wretched,
Affection, duty, every thing will yield
To love and Mortimer —

Mort. No Adelaide I shall try to hide my misery;
This sacrifice ic due to gratitude;
DeCourcy shall receive the life which his humanity
                                        preserved.   40
For think not I can ever live, to see thee made an
                                        other's,
At present virtue bids me fly —
My Adelaide farewell for ever —

Adel. Oh will you leave me when I most need a friend?

Mort. Does Adelaide bid me stay?

Adel: Indeed you must not go;
For my poor heart is almost burst already,
And that would break it quite;
Duty doth but feebly resist
Such powerful love as mine —   50

Mort. Away then sorrow, and each gloomy care,
Since Adelaide loves me still, I've nought to fear

Adel—Duty calls me one way, love another,

Between the two my peace is lost for ever —
Away — My father comes;
He must not see you here.

Mort. My dearest love, my Adelaide adieu;
But tho' I go my heart is still with you — *Exit.*

Adel: What shall I say! I cannot bear his anger —

Enter De Courcy

De C. Still, Still in tears, and why?   60
Because I wish to make you happy —
Once Adelaide I thought I had a child
Who would not thus have vexed her parents' heart
But now I find how great was the mistake.

Adel. Oh! My father, look not on me thus:
That frown will kill me —

De C. Adelaide, I beg, entreat you,
If you ever loved me,
If you regard your future happiness,
Now by your conduct show it;   70
But if you still refuse my only prayer
For once I must command;
If Adelaide forgets she is my child,
I shall forget it too —
And act a tyrant's part —

Adel. Had you commanded me aught else on earth,
Were it to die I'd willingly obey:

To this, and this alone, I never can consent;
Horatio's misfortunes, virtues, and his youth,
Have gained him my esteem;   80
But more I cannot give —
Then my loved father on my bended knees, (Kneeling[)]
Let me entreat you,
Not to make your child for ever wretched —

De C. I'll hear no more; your prayers all are in vain;
My word is past; nor shall a woman's tears
Make me recall it —
Mark well my words,
Or you'll repent this obstinacy,
And violence shall obtain what duty ought to give   90
                                                    Exit —

Adel. Open thou earth and hide me from his anger —
Oh! Mortimer when my poor father found thee
Deserted and forlorn upon the shore
A helpless Babe,
He little thought that thou shouldst be the cause
Of so much misery to my poor heart —
I'll seek Horatio,
And throw myself upon his goodness,
(My last remaining hope). Exit —

             Scene III An apartment in Horatio's House
                    Enter Horatio & Oreztan —

Horatio —
Oreztan I do fear me much,

Your health agrees not with the English clime
And now indeed I do repent me,
That I e'er yielded to your rash request,
To bring me with you from your native land —

Orez: The Sorrows of a Heart with woe o'erpowered
And not the clime, affect my health Horatio
And Oh! where can I hope that They will cease?
If not in England —

Hor: Your words are still mysterious,   10
Nor do I seek to know their meaning,
For oft with pain I have observed,
When I e'er touched upon your life o'erpast —
The very thought seemed to harrass your Soul;
But you have left your Country, all, for me;
Sure then each care that friendship can bestow,
Must need be yours —

Orez: By Our Prophet I do know thee well,
And know the generous nature
Of thy manly breast;   20
But my griefs are not like to those of other men
And therefore undisclosed they must remain,
Until the time that fate reveal them —
But let me beg
That thou wilt say no more upon this subject;
How stand your hopes with Adelaide?

Hor: Would I could say well!
But tho. her father doth assist my suit,

She herself is still, as ever, cold;
But yet I hope and trust she may relent —   30
Now to the Castle let us bend our way,
I fear to see her, yet I dare not stay

                        Exeunt —

        Scene 4 — A garden near the Castle
            Enter Mortimer —

Mort: All nature seems to mourn for Adelaide's woes:
      Why do I say for Adelaide's?
      Are not my own as great?
      Oh! Yes — and greater far;
      But in her tears my sorrows are forgot.
      The Birds have ceased to tune their joyous strain,
      And plaintive notes express their sympathy;
      The Sun has sunk beneath the lowering clouds,   40
      Which sprinkle all around with pitying tears;
      The roses droop and wither in their bloom —
      A mournful emblem of my hapless love —

                      Enter Stanmore
Stan "Hapless love" — what means this said complaint?
      Has the fair shrine which humbly you adore
      Refused to grant what vows and prayers seek?
      Or has some young, some pretty sighing fool
      Woo'd the inconstant fair one from your arms,
      And triumphed in a heart not worth the having?

Mort: Cease Stanmore to profane,   50
      With a blaspheming tongue,
      The truest, loveliest, best of women —

Stan: Lovely she is; but true she cannot be;
      Or if she is indeed, why then, she is the first
      That e'er beneath an Angel's form
      Concealed an Angel's mind —
      I have abjured them all;
      For all are treacherous alike —

Mort: Oh No! My Adelaide is excellence itself —

Stan: So I once thought Zalniora;   60
      She too was lovely and I thought her true;
      But oh! how fatally was I deceived —
      When first my eyes beheld the beauteous slave
      My heart confessed her charms more powerful far

                    [fragment ends here]

2

[MY LOVED MINSTREL]

Still my loved Minstrel I admire
The strains of thy enchanted lyre
Still thy sad lays so wildly sweet
I read — and while I read I weep
Nor do I check the burning tear   5
For 'tis a silent tribute dear
To Souls like thine which would inspire
Each breast with sympathetic fire
Byron thy noble lofty mind
Has been the sport of passions blind   10
Phrenzy has havocked in thy brain
With all her desolating train
But that is past — and now you roam
Far from your wife — your child your home
Joys which might still have been your own   15
But shall I love my Byron less
Because he knows not happiness
Ah no — tho' worlds condemn him now
Though sharp tongued fame has sunk him low
The hapless wanderer still must be   20
Pitied, revered, adored by me.

3
[I LOVE THE MOUNTAIN TORRENT]

I love the mountain torrent dashing,
Downward, in thunder loud, and hoarse,
With snow-white foam, in fury, lashing
The rugged rocks that break its course —
I love the thunder, rumbling, crashing,   5
Peal after peal along the skies,
While from the clouds, the lightning flashing
In death-ful splendour, strikes — destroys —

I love the soul no danger fearing,
Still onward rushing to its goal,   10
All that impedes its course down-bearing,
Proud, fiery, broking no control.
I love the conqu'ror's name declaring
In its wild sound, the will of fate,
Still followed by some deed of daring,   15
That makes astounded empires quake —

4
THE WISH

Oh for a valley far away!
Where human foot hath never been,
Where sunbeams ever brightly play,
And all is young, and fresh, and green.

Oh for a valley far away!   5
    Where human tongue ne'er utter'd sound
Where envy, hate, and treachery
    Have never yet an entrance found.

Where cunning never spread her wile;
    Where passion's fever never burn'd,   10
Making the heart a fun'ral pile
    Of hopes to desolation burn'd —

Where nature only sees for tears,
    The dewy drops, by Morning shed;
When with a Mother's love she cheers   15
    The little flowret's drooping head —

Where nature only hears for sighs
    The balm that gentle Zephyr breathes;
When through the scented grove he flies
    Kissing the dew drops from its leaves —   20

There could I spend my peaceful days,
    With only *one* my lot to share;
One in whose soul depths I might gaze,
    And see my thoughts reflected there.

With one who car'd for none but me, 25
    Whose looks of love were all my own;
Whose heart would for my image be
    A living tomb when I am gone.

Is this the destiny that I desire?
Oh no! I'm infinitely better here; 30
I verily believe I should expire,
If doom'd to solitude a single year;
'Tis well there was no evil Fairy near,
To grant immediately what'ere I chose;
Or, for my wishing, I had paid as dear, 35
As that poor man who (as the story goes)
Attach'd a long, black pudding to his spouse's nose —

5

LINES TO LORD BYRON
From his daughter, Ada

Father! what love that word reveals!
    What dreams of bliss to me unknown!
Sweet sound! my inmost soul it thrills,
    Like music's saddest, wildest tone.

Father! Ah! word pronounced in vain!   5
    He hears not — echo only hears —
For ever must I breathe that name,
    Gayless as now — alone — in tears.

They tell me oft his cold neglect
    Should all my early love efface;   10
Would they could teach me to forget
    His parting look, his last embrace!

And oft they chide the tear that fills
    My eye while list'ning to his fame,
The thought of pride my bosom thrills,   15
    "I am his child! — I bear his name!"

In vain they blame: they are his foes,
    He did them wrong — they've cause to hate!
But in my breast the life that glows
    Is his — for me to love him's fate.   20

Oh, still, my Father, joy will steal
    Bright on my soul; while all alone

I read thy words of fire, and feel
 Thine cannot be a heart of stone.

I dream each day may end my pain,   25
 That thou, ev'n thou, canst cease to hate;
That foreign charms may lure in vain,
 And home be dear for Ada's sake.

Deceitful hopes! my years roll on
 And each new day is like the past;   30
Still, still I live unloved, alone,
 Ah! this fond heart will break at last!

6
VERSES WRITTEN AT MIDNIGHT

The sun has left the skies
    And pass'd the azure waves,
And now reposing lies
    In ocean's hidden caves;
A veil of darkness shrouds   5
    The bright and lovely dome
Of gold and crimson clouds,
    Where late his glory shone.

From silver throne on high
    The pale, cold queen of night   10
Irradiates the sky
    With melancholy light.
While all the world's asleep,
    Alone I wake to gaze
On that cold moon, and weep,   15
    And think of other days.

The night-wind moans around
    And wakes the wild harp's tone.
So mournful is that sound
    'Twould thrill a heart of stone.   20
It dies upon the blast,
    And now it wildly swells, —
The spirit of the past
    Amid such music dwells.

How wild the pang we feel   25
    In such an hour as this!
When o'er the spirit steal
    The thoughts of vanished bliss.
Of friends in early youth
    When, unsuspecting guile,   30
We thought kind words were truth,
    And trusted every smile.

Of some we once believed
    Could ne'er have been estranged,
Whose fondness hath deceived,   35
    Whose hearts and looks are changed;
Of others who have crossed
    Our path — friends of a day —
That scarcely loved, e'er lost,
    Like dreams have passed away.   40

7
LINES — ON I DON'T KNOW WHAT

Too quickly art thou vanished dream of youth!
Fair, sunbright dream! by which a while deceiv'd,
My soul was gay amidst life's dismal truth,
(Sorrow and disappointment) now conceiv'd
Its happiness delusion; but believ'd   5
That fair ideal world could remain,
Tho' death was all around — Tho' now bereav'd
Of its gay hopes it seeks tho past in pain!
The dream of youth once dreamt doth ne'er return again.

Life! life! upon my heart thy sadness lies   10
Like the icy hand of death; my eye in vain
Though all condition of existence flies,
And finds not one that is exempt from pain
But man, deluded man still hugs the chain
That binds him down to love; still eager tries,   15
Though various disappointment to attain.
The fair deceitful phantom happiness
That ever flees his grasp, till in pursuit — he dies.

Oh! what is all that mortals most esteem?
Power, riches, honours are but gilded woe;   20
And pleasure is a short-liv'd fev'rish dream,
That leaves regret when it hath ceas'd to glow;
The flower of *love* is rarely seen to blow;
Beauty is but the splendid garb of death;
And FAME of all possessions, here below,   25
The best, the brightest, is an empty breath;
Alas! where is the one true charm existence hath?

Oh fancy hide from me life's dismal waste!
Let thy bright [orisons] o'er my spirit steal!
The wretch upon the rack hath leave to taste   30
A Moment of repose; tho' but to feel
His agonies the more; then come reveal
The scenes, the happiness fate hath not giv'n
To sons of earth (it may be) for their weal;
For if the soul had ne'er with anguish striv'n.   35
Ah! could it hope in death, or waft one wish to heav'n.

8

[THE SETTING SUN]

See how the setting sun adorns the plain,
With splendid rays of gold and crimson hue!
Where is the noble heart that does not glow,
With new-born rapture at so fair a scene?
Look to the stars! how beautiful they shine!   5
How musical the murm'ring waters flow!
Surely an Emp'ror hath his garden here!
The carpets of the King of Morning glow
With many brilliant hues; but these gay fields
Are with more rich and varied colours dy'd;   10
The air is full of musk; the stream exhales
Ottar of roses; jessamine that bows
Beneath a load of flowers, rose-trees that breathe
Odours around, these are the garden-gods —
There struts the Pheasant of his plumage proud,   15
And here the nightingale and turtle-dove
Timid descend upon the cypress boughs.
Far as the eye can reach along the stream,
It rests on paradise. The hills, and plains
Are cover'd with young girls angel-bright.   20
No wonder Man is happy where [Menischeh],
The daughter of [Afrasiab] appears;
'Tis she who makes this garden beautiful,
And brilliant as the sun; child of a king.
A new-born Star! 'tis she who hath diffus'd   25
This richness, and this spendour o'er the plain,
Above the rose and jessamine she shines;
Beauty unequal'd! her bright face is veil'd,

But the cypress equals not her form in grace;
Her mouth exhales a cloud of amber round her,   30
On her fair cheeks roses repose; her eyes
Are dark, and full of sleep; her parted lips
Are colour'd like pure-wine, and their perfume!
His the rose's essence! Would to God!
That we could reach that dwelling place of bliss.   35
Would that it were the journey of a day! —

9

[WITH SONG AND DANCE GROTESQUE]

With Song and Dance grotesque, Historians say
The Jews, did homage to the ark display!
We Christians, more refined, do pious airs,
And holy Anthems, mingle with our prayers.

No more distorted gestures now we see   5
But show devotion on our bended knee!
Meek, tho' sincere our orisons should rise
To Him, who sits enthroned above the skies.

Let ev'ry note in harmony accord
When we in Song address the living Lord: 10
And silence, with her eloquent control
Give Music grace, to elevate the Soul.

With Song and Dance grotesque, Historians say
The Jews, did homage to the ark display!
We Christians, more refined, do pious airs,
And holy Anthems, mingle with our prayers

No more distorted gestures now we see
But shew devotion on our bended knee!
Meek, tho' sincere our orisons should rise
To Him, who sits enthroned above the skies

Let ev'ry note in harmony accord
When we in Song address the living Lord:
And science, with her elegant control
Give music grace, to elevate the Soul

J Welsh

[With Song and Dance Grotesque]
Courtesy of the National Library of Scotland

10
[DARK CHAIN]

Dark Chain I clasp thee round my neck with pride
A Poet's present to a Poet's bride;
If ill such metal suit so gay a face,
And charm of shining gold might better grace,
I know what graces more than that or this   5
A heart to make and feel another's bliss.

11
[NAY, THIS IS HOPE]

Nay, this is Hope: a gentle dove,
    That nestles in the gentle breast,
Bringing glad tidings from above
    Of joys to come and heavenly rest.

And this is Life: ethereal fire   5
    Striving aloft through smothering clay;
Mounting, flaming, higher, higher!
    Till lost in immortality.

And Man — oh! hate not nor despise
    The fairest, lordliest work of God!   10
Think not He made the good and wise
    Only to sleep beneath the sod!

The Translations of Jane Welsh Carlyle

1
THE FISHER

1.

The water rush'd the water swell'd
   A Fisher sat thereby;
He looked upon the rod he held,
   His heart was full of joy.

2.

His eye he gave, his ear he gave   5
   To watch the flowing stream;
When lo! above the parted wave
   A water-nymph was seen.

3.

She softly spoke, she softly sang,
   "Ah cruel! wherefore wish   10
With wit of man and wiles of man
   To lure my harmless fish?

4.

"Couldst thou but know how merrily
   The Trout plays in the deep,
Thou wouldst go with me speedily   15
   His cool abode to seek.

5.

"Doth not the Moon, doth not the Sun
   In ocean love to bathe?
And do they not more bright become
   When they have breath'd the wave?   20

6.

"Doth that deep Heaven lure thee not
   That wave of lucid blue?
Doth thine own image lure thee not
   Into eternal dew?"

7.

The water rush'd, the water swell'd,   25
   It lav'd his naked foot;
His heart with fond desire was fill'd
   As at love's soft salute.

8.

She spoke to him, she sang to him
   His love of earth was o'er   30
With gentle force she drew him in
   He ne'er was heard of more.

2
An Indian Mother's Lament

My new-born Babe! why doth thy Mother weep,
In grief to see thee cradled in thy tomb?
The little bird when grown hath food to seek,
And in the desert bitter grains are found! —
Thine eyes have not known tears, nor hath thy heart   5
To Man's destroying breath yet been exposed.
The fragrant rose that withers in the bud,
With all its sweet perfume doth pass away,
As thou, my Boy, with all thine innocence.
Ah! thou art happy! thou hast only known   10
A Mother's kisses and a Mother's smiles.

3
A LOVE SONG

As one who longs for cooling drink,
The cruel fires of thirst to quench,
When haply on one verdant branch
He saw two apples, stays to think
Which may be best, and both desires: 5
So was I by two maids perplexed;
But now at last my choice is fixed;
And one true love my soul inspires.

As Ocean foams and harshly roars
When two fierce winds assail his breast,   10
In fearful strife from east and west;
Nor ever to repose restores
His waves till one is overthrown;
So by two flames my soul assailed
Raged till the fiercest flame prevailed;   15
And now I live for thee alone.

4
[FROM EAST TO WEST]

From east to west let it be told,
I'll give the honest lumps of gold,
If all the rascals will agree,
To pay, each one, a pin to me;
I will without delay pay down,   5
To ev'ry man of sense a crown,
If all the silly fools that live,
Will each to me a farthing give —

I could write down upon my thumb
The good that half mankind have done;   10
And all the wisdom I have heard,
Would scarcely fill a calling-card —
A pigeon's wing would be enough,
To feed all who are men of worth;
But would you give the knaves a treat,   15
You may cry 'come, good folks, and eat!'

Notes to the Poems of Thomas Carlyle

1
Tragedy of the Night-Moth

Commentary: "Tragedy of the Night-Moth" is Carlyle's earliest ex-
tant poem. Included in the "Fractions," all of which were dated
1823-1833 by Carlyle, it seems certain to have been written much
earlier, perhaps as early as 1817. In a letter to Jane, dated Oc-
tober, 1822, Carlyle writes, "What put it into your imagination
that our unhappy Night-moth was translated? Alas! the poor
animal actually perished before my eyes one summer midnight
in the Burgh of Kirkcaldy; and like Jerry of the Carlisle news-
paper, I *pat eet aw into langish meesel'*. This lest Posterity should
mistake the thing" (*Letters*, II, 189). Carlyle taught school in
Kirkcaldy from November, 1816, to the fall of 1818 when he
resigned and returned to Edinburgh. Alexander Carlyle dates the
poem from this period, 1818 (*Love Letters*, I, 94n.). As G. B.
Tennyson observes, the reference to Goethe in the poem argues
for a somewhat later date, since Carlyle did not begin his study
of German until 1819, and thus would not have known Goethe's
work in the original before then. However, as Tennyson notes, the
poem was a personal favorite of Carlyle's, and the reference to
Goethe might well be an emendation dating much later ("Poetry,"
p. 167n.). Tennyson's observation gains credence when it is
considered that a copy of the poem apparently was sent to Goethe
himself and that the poem was first published in 1830 in *Chaos*,
a weekly coterie journal published in Weimar by Goethe's daugh-
ter-in-law Ottilie and her circle.[1] Subsequently, Carlyle published
the poem in *Fraser's* (August, 1831), corrected that printing
(with pencil revisions) in *Original Reviews*, and included the poem
in the first and subsequent editions of the *Essays*. It was the
only one of his poems included in the first edition of the *Essays*.
Composition: [1818?].
Manuscript: Untraced.
First Publication: *Chaos*, I, No. 32 [1830], 126-127.
Texts Consulted: *Chaos*, *Fraser's*, IV, No. 19 (August, 1831), 64;
     Original Reviews; *Essays*, 1st ed. (1838), III, 43-45; *Essays*, 2nd
     ed. (1840), III, 262-264; *Essays*, People's Edition (1872), VI (Vol.
     I of *Critical and Miscellaneous Essays*), 287-288.
Copy-text: *Essays*, 2nd ed.

Gloss: *Magna ausus*: 'having dared great things.'

Textual Notes: Although no manuscript of "Tragedy of the Night-Moth" seems to have survived, Alexander Carlyle reported in 1909 that a copy of the poem in Jane Carlyle's handwriting was sent to Weimar and was still preserved in the Goethe archives there (*Love Letters,* I, 95n.).   The Goethe-Schiller Archiv can now find no trace of the manuscript.   Presumably this lost manuscript was the one that provided the text for the *Chaos* issue, which is signed "I. C. [,]" no doubt a misprint for "J. C.," Jane Carlyle.   Also the *Chaos* version is dated "Edinb. 1813 [,]" but in light of Carlyle's recollection of where, and therefore when, the inspirational event occurred, the *Chaos* date must be a misprint or misreading for "1818."   The printed version from *Fraser's* that Carlyle had bound for Jane, here titled *Original Reviews,* contains pencilled revisions to lines 3 and 4 in Carlyle's hand, making the text of these lines conform to the *Chaos* version.   The first edition of the *Essays* (Boston, 1838), which was initiated by Emerson and edited by Charles Stearns Wheeler and Henry S. McKean, reprints the *Fraser's* text without substantive changes.   The second edition of the *Essays* (London, 1840) is the first over which Carlyle seems to have exercised direct authorial control.

Variants:

3   for knowledge seeking] his studies seeking (*Chaos, Original Reviews*); all things are sleeping (*Fraser's*)
4   All mortal things to sleep are]His mind to study still is (*Fraser's*)
12   Fount] fount (*Chaos, Fraser's*)
16   and — puff!] — and puff! (*Chaos*); ,and — puff! (People's Edition)
20   snaps and] snaps — and (*Chaos*)
29   thee,] thee. (*Chaos*)
32   earth] Earth (*Chaos*)
33   Space] space (*Chaos, Fraser's*)
34   thee!] thee, (*Chaos*)
35   unheeded,] unheeded (*Chaos*, People's Edition)
36   little] slender (*Chaos, Fraser's*)
38   earth] Earth (*Chaos, Fraser's*)
39   frame] frame, (People's Edition)
40   earth] Earth (*Chaos, Fraser's*)
44   good] Good (*Chaos, Fraser's*)

45   lot] hap (*Chaos*)

48   date!] date. (*Chaos*)

55   thoughts like these,]   with'ring thought (*Chaos*); withering thoughts (*Fraser's*)

56   deep, are — death more slow!] deep — are but a death more slow. (*Chaos*); deep, are but a death more slow. (*Fraser's*)

Citations:

[1] The issues of *Chaos* are not dated but are numbered; hence dates can be accurately inferred by counting weeks and numbers. *Chaos* was published from August, 1829, through early 1832, interrupted from October, 1830, to the summer of 1831 because of the death of Ottilie's husband August. See Reinhard Fink, "Das 'Chaos' und seine Mitarbeiter," bound with a reprint of *Chaos* in *Chaos: Herausgegeben von Ottilie von Goethe unter Einschluss der Fortsetzungen Création und Creation* (Bern: Herbert Lang, 1968), pp. 44-45. For further discussion of Carlyle's link to *Chaos*, see Goethe's letter to Carlyle dated 14 June, 1830 (*Letters*, V, 160) and Trevor D. Jones, "English Contributors to Ottilie von Goethe's 'Chaos,'" *English Goethe Society*, 9 (1931-1933), 66-89.

2

Peter Nimmo

Commentary: "Peter Nimmo" is Carlyle's longest poem and is of uncertain date. David Masson assigned the poem to "before 1821" because he felt that the phrase "in heath and splashy weather" in the prologue seemed to indicate that the poem was composed while Carlyle was in Annandale.[1] David Wilson gave 1822 as a likely date (*Carlyle Till Marriage*, p. 265), and G. B. Tennyson tentatively agrees with Wilson's date (*Sartor*, p. 333). A date of 1824 is also possible, the year that Carlyle wrote a short piece for the university magazine *The Lapsus Linguae* on Nimmo. Carlyle's first mention of the poem appears in a letter to Henry Inglis that is dated 15 June, 1830, where Carlyle asks about other Edinburgh personalities and "Peter Nimmo also, on whom I have a Poem, written for you . . ." (*Letters*, V, 115). The poem could thus date from 1830 or any time prior, but since its locale and subject center on the university, a date in the early twenties seems likely for first composition.

Pressed for funds and casting about for publishable material, Carlyle writes to his brother John on 19 October, 1830, and asks, "Did you ever see a rhapsody of mine (in verse) called Peter Nimmo, and think you it would suit Fraser?" (*Letters,* V, 175-176). Later, in November, he submitted the poem along with "The Beetle," "Schiller," and the manuscript "On Clothes" (the germ of *Sartor Resartus*) to *Fraser's,* where the poem was published along with a prose introduction in February, 1831.[2] This printing in *Fraser's* was the only publication of the poem in Carlyle's lifetime.

David Masson provides the only account of the historical Peter Nimmo and describes him as "a lank, miserable, mendicant-looking object, of unknown age, with a blue face, often scarred and patched, and garments not of the cleanest, the chief of which was a long, threadbare, snuff-brown great-coat."[3]   Peter Nimmo appears to have come to the University of Edinburgh around the turn of the century to train for the ministry and then to have abandoned serious pursuit of a degree in favor of attending various classes over many years until he became an object of local color and humor.   Masson reports, for instance, that in 1810-1811 Nimmo was in the mathematics and logic classes with Carlyle, that he was Carlyle's classmate in Leslie's mathematical class in 1811-1812, that in 1813-1814 he was registered in the eighth year of his literary course, and that in 1819-1820, when Carlyle was attending the Scots Law Class, Peter Nimmo was attending two of the medical classes, having entered himself in the matriculation book as being in the seventeenth year of his theological studies (pp. 287-288).   Masson also quotes Hill Burton's estimate of Nimmo in 1830-1831: "merely an idly-inclined and stupidish man of low condition, who having once got into practice as a sort of public laughing-stock, saw that the occupation paid better than honest industry, and had cunning enough to keep it up" (pp. 286-287).   Finally, Masson notes that Nimmo was known for calling at various houses to obtain meals, that he used to boast of his high family, and that he was still a fixture around University environs as late as 1846 in Masson's own memory.

Composition: [1818-1830].

Manuscript: Yale University (watermark 1827).

First Publication: *Fraser's Magazine,* III, No. 13 (February, 1831), 12-16.

Texts Consulted: MS; *Fraser's*; *Original Reviews*.
Copy-text: MS.
Glosses:

  Rhapsody: The *OED* defines rhapsody as, among other things,
    'an epic poem or part of one'; 'a miscellaneous collection;
    a medley or confused mass' ; and 'an exalted or exageratedly
    enthusiastic expression of sentiment or feeling; an effusion . . .
    marked by extravagance of idea and expression, but without
    connected thought or sound argument.' Carlyle also called
    Sartor Resartus a "Rhapsody" in a letter to Emerson dated
    13 May, 1835; see *The Correspondence of Emerson and Car-
    lyle,* ed. Joseph Slater (New York: Columbia University Press,
    1964), p. 129.

  Numeris fertur lege solutis: 'He is borne along in numbers un-
    fettered by law'; Horace, *Caramina*, IV, 2, 11, referring to
    Pindar's "hobbling" meter.

2   *Scribendi cacoethes*: 'itch for writing'; Juvenal, *Satire* 7, 52.

30   *bush*: The *OED* gives one definition of *bush* as 'a branch or
      bunch of ivy (perhaps as the plant sacred to Bacchus) hung
      up as a vintner's sign; *hence,* the sign-board of a tavern.'

30   *mild penny-wheep*: Scottish dialect for the weakest kind of
      small beer.

39   τιμή : (noun) 'worship,' 'esteem,' 'honor.'

46   *Delphic Tripod*: The golden tripod was placed over the
      mouth of the cave at Delphi whence the prophetic vapor rose
      The priestess of Apollo sat on the tripod, caught the inspira-
      tion, and pronounced oracles in extemporaneous prose or
      verse.

61   *hest*: 'purpose.'

71   *Cuddy*: Dumfriesshire dialect for 'ass.'

72   "*butter-and-eggs*": a short jigging trot.

85   "*blue-bore*": an opening showing blue sky through clouds.

131   *prog*: college slang for 'food.'

133   *reek*: 'smoke.'

135   *gabble*: 'chatter.'

144   *marrow*: 'equal.'

149   *menstruum*: a slovent, or any liquid by which a solid may be
      dissolved.

155   *variorum*: The *OED* cites a figurative use of *variorum* as
      'Variation; a varying or changing scene' and gives the fol-
      lowing from Burns' *Jolly Beggars* as an illustration: "Life
      is all a variorum, We regard not how it goes."

Textual Notes: An undated manuscript of "Peter Nimmo" is among
the "Twenty-four manuscript poems" at Yale University, and
J. A. S. Barrett's notes that accompany these poems attribute
the manuscript to 1831 and judge it to be a copy; Barrett agrees
with Masson, however, that the original poem was composed much
earlier and suggests between 1818-1824 as the likely period.
The manuscript, watermarked 1827, is not the printer's copy for
the *Fraser's* printing, but the text of the manuscript and that of
the *Fraser's* printing do not differ radically.   What substantive
differences do exist suggest that the manuscript precedes the
Fraser's text: for example, the manuscript has Peter Nimmo
haunting the university for twenty-three years whereas the poem
and the prose introduction in *Fraser's* both give twenty-five years.
The *Fraser's* printing was included without changes in *Original
Reviews*.

   Although the fact that the manuscript appears to represent
an earlier state of the poem and that Carlyle included the *Fraser's*
version in *Original Reviews* might give some support to the choice
of the *Fraser's* text as copy-text, one cannot accept the absence of
revisions in the *Original Reviews* volume as conclusive evidence of
final intention.   Carlyle did not revise accidentals of any of the
poems included in *Original Reviews,* and only "Tragedy of the
Night-Moth" contains substantive revisions; however, *all* of the
poems that were subsequently published in his works appear in
different forms there than appear in *Original Reviews*.   In addition,
Carlyle had sent the manuscript of the poem to his brother John
in London and had previously instructed James Fraser that John
was to revise any proofsheets (*Letters*, V, 128).   For these reasons
the Yale manuscript has been followed for accidentals except
in rare instances where the *Fraser's* version seems to reflect legit-
imate authorial revision, and all substantive changes found in the
Fraser's text have been incorporated except those that seem to
result from a misreading of the manuscript (for example, "jolting"
for "jotting").   With the exception of spelling corrections, all
emendations of copy-text are reported in the list of emendations,
but only substantive variants are included in the list of variants.
Emendations:
   Peter Nimmo] The manuscript is simply titled RHAPSODY.
   15   Must the brain] Nay, must brain

17   living Man] Man of soul
17   twice-sold] tench or
19   wonder-fill'd] full of wonders
19   for instance] *e.g.*
28   meekly] mildly
30   "mild penny-wheep"] 'mild penny-wheep'
43   five] three
44   Class-rooms] Classes
61   hest:] hest
62   nowise will appear.] not the least appear
65]   Live men-like fish, their creel this earthly Ball
99   that soul's] the mind's
101   sheen] light
103   deign] say
105   dost] does
106]   (Tho' driving no whit but dragged).
149   menstruum),] menstruum)
163   sure 'tis Peter,] sure 'tis Peter
Variants:
6   Letters] letters (*Fraser's*)
13   Matters not] In the manuscript "it" is cancelled following
        "matters[,]" and "whit" is cancelled following "not[.]"
15   ?];
20   myst'ry] The word was originally "mystery"; the *e* is can-
        celled and an apostrophe added. *Fraser's* prints "mystery[.]"
32]   This replaces a cancelled line between lines 31 and 32 in the
        manuscript; "In an eager, short, half-hurried trudge" original-
        ly; "To all class-rooms" then added in the margin to left
        and cancelled.
34]   "of thine" is interpolated above the line in the manuscript,
        and a caret is placed below the line and following "head[.]"
37   beat'st] bear'st
45   jotting] jolting
54]   "thereto" is cancelled in the manuscript following "leisure
        [.]"
56]   "Mid" is cancelled in the manuscript before "wondrous"
        and is replaced by "Rose" added in the left margin.
64   diving] Diving
66   ?] !

69   nowhere] no where
72   butter] Butter
77   Kirk] kirk
88   hand and *un*arm'd] *un*arm'd
93   grammar] Grammar-
94]   "wh" is cancelled in the manuscript following "trottest—"
99   aurora] Aurora
100   Gates] gates
101   thee] ye
104]   "Ay Young (tho" is the cancelled original beginning of the
       line in the manuscript and is written between lines 103 and
       104.
123   he!] he?
145   He] he
VI   *L'Envoy*] not numbered in *Fraser's*

Citations:

[1]Masson, p. 291.

[2]Tennyson argues that the prose introduction was written in
1830 for the publication of the poem in *Fraser's* and that this
introduction has caused some critics to interpret the poem as a
sort of precursor to *Sartor Resartus,* with Peter Nimmo as its
hero (Tennyson, *Sartor,* pp. 62-65). Heinrich Kraeger and Arthur
Mämpel take this view and see Nimmo as a misunderstood and
tragic figure who goes to the university to learn, but who is offered
only empty formulas there ("Carlyles Stellung zur Deutschen
Sprache und Literatur," *Anglia,* 22 [1899], 169 and *Thomas
Carlyle als Künstler* [Göttingen: Göttingen University Press,
1935], p. 59, respectively).

[3]Masson, pp. 285-288.   Masson's account of Peter Nimmo is
followed throughout.

3

The Wish

Commentary: "The Wish" is the first of the courtship poems and
     probably dates from the summer of 1822. On 27 May, 1822,
     Carlyle writes to Jane proposing that they alternately prescribe
     subjects that they might both write on and suggests "The Wish"

as the subject for their first attempt: "The most plausible task
I can hit upon is a little article to be entitled *The Wish*, where-
in we are to set forth respectively the kind of fate and condition
we most long for — and have some feeble expectation of attain-
ing" (*Letters*, II, 116). Jane responds in mid-June with "my wish
. . . the most foolish little thing possible" (*Letters*, II, 130); upon
which Carlyle comments in his reply of about 17 June, "Your
'Wish' is quite an emblem of your usual treacherous disposition.
. . . You are growing a delightful romantic character — alive to
all the simple enjoyments of existence" (*Letters*, II, 131). Jane
found the subject of Carlyle's poem here "so touchingly imaged"
(*Letters*, IV, 59).

Composition: [May-June, 1822].

Manuscript: Untraced.

First Publication: *Leigh Hunt's London Journal*, No. 35 (26 November,
1834), 280.

Texts Consulted: *Leigh Hunt's London Journal*; *Love Letters*, II, 347-
348.

Copy-text: *Leigh Hunt's London Journal*.

Textual Notes: The poem is signed "T" in *Leigh Hunt's London
Journal* and was first identified as Carlyle's by Alexander Car-
lyle in 1909, when he also noted that the manuscript had been
lost prior to that time (*Love Letters*, II, 348n.). The text printed
in *Love Letters* is presumedly that from *Leigh Hunt's London
Journal* since Alexander Carlyle states that the printed copy that
he found among Jane's portfolio materials was a newspaper cut-
ting. On the slim chance, however, that the single variant in *Love
Letters* represents a later authorial revision, the variant is given
below.

Variant:

39 must] may (*Love Letters*)

4

With the Bramah's Pen

Commentary: Barrett's notes suggest that "With the Bramah's Pen"
was written in 1823, but the poem was almost certainly written
to accompany a pen that Carlyle sent as a gift along with some

books to Jane on 9 August, 1822. In the letter that went with the gifts he writes, "There is also a miserable pen — which upon examination I find *not* to be one of Bramah's, or worth a single doit; accompanied with some doggrel which is worth even less" (*Letters,* II, 155-156).

Composition: [August, 1822].

Manuscript: Yale University.

First Publication: Unpublished.

Texts Consulted: MS.

Copy-text: MS.

Gloss:

> *Bramah*: *The Dictionary of National Biography* lists Joseph Bramah (1748-1814) as an inventor whose specialty was perfecting other people's inventions for the most part and who was known in his own day primarily for his improved water closet, padlock, and hydraulic press. Among the number of his minor inventions was "the ever-pointed pencil."

Textual Notes: The undated manuscript at Yale provides the only text for "With the Bramah's Pen." The title is underlined twice in the manuscript.

Emendations:

> 16 another's] anothers
> 24 ages.] ages

Variant:

> 25 fears and] In the manuscript this is written above the line, and a caret is placed below the line and following "thy [.] "

5

Morgarten

Commentary: Begun in September of 1822, "Morgarten" is Carlyle's only surviving poem on a historical subject and probably grew out of his occupation with Schiller's *Wilhelm Tell*.[1] He writes to Jane on 11 September that he had "tried rhyming repeatedly, but it would not answer. Once I had reached the third stanza of a hymn on the Battle of Morgarten . . ." (*Letters,* II, 161-162). His only other mention of the poem appears in a letter written to his mother on 4 December in which he enclosed a copy of the poem: "I send you a small *screed* of verses, which I made sometime ago: I fear you will not care a doit for them, tho' the subject is good — the deliverance of Switzerland from tyranny by the hardy mountaineers at the battle of Morgarten some five hundred years ago" (*Letters,* II, 219).

Composition: [September, 1822].

Manuscript: Yale University.

First Publication: Froude (1882), I, 172-173.

Texts Consulted: MS; Froude.

Copy-text: MS.

Gloss:

Morgarten: The incident that the poem recounts occurred on 15 November, 1315, when a mail-clad Austrian force under Duke Leopold attacked the rebelling Waldstatte, a league formed of the three forest cantons of Uri, Schwyz, and Unterwalden. Unable to charge because of the confines of the terrain, the Austrians were soundly defeated by defenders hurling boulders from the mountain slopes, and the defeat marked the practical end of Hapsburg rule in Switzerland.

Textual Notes: The undated Yale manuscript provides the only text of the poem that carries authorial sanction. Froude has come in for considerable criticism regarding his editorial habits, and his text cannot be trusted with much confidence. His printing of the poem contains some thirty variants in substantives and accidentals; but since it is remotely possible that he may have been working from a different manuscript, his substantive variants are listed below.

Emendation:

19   Despot] Froude; Depot

Variants:

4   their] the (Froude)
8   Nations] nation
10   The stern voice] The voice
10   arose?] arose,
11   their glen] the glen
12   foes?] foes.
13   fell] Fell
14   men!] men;
15   times] time

22   Horror] horrour
23   glow] grow,

Citation:

[1]Arthur Mämpel, *Thomas Carlyle als Künstler* (Göttingen: Göttingen University Press, 1935), p. 46.

6
[They Chide Thee, Fair and Fervid One]

Commentary: Alexander Carlyle dated this poem and believed it to have been enclosed with an incomplete letter of 22 December, 1823, that Carlyle sent to Jane after he had returned from a visit to Edinburgh and a stopover to visit Jane (*Love Letters,* I, 316n.). This was rather a time of turmoil for both Carlyle and Jane as winter was setting in, he was staying with the Bullers at Kinnaird House and suffering from dyspepsia (one of the reasons for his trip was to seek medical treatment), and Jane was unhappy with her social life at Haddington. Part of Carlyle's letter reads as follows:

> I do not recollect that I ever thought more, or more anxiously, about you than since we parted last. It still seems to my alarmed imagination that the crisis of our fate is at hand, that we are to be dashed asunder by the strong arms of Destiny, and driven ere long into everlasting separation. In fact it is clear enough that things cannot stand as they are. For me I have long looked on pitiful Misery as my companion for life; there is little hope of my recovering even health, and without this the sceptre of the universe were not worth a pin. So I have laid my account with endurance and a perpetual train of despicable suffering — till the end — which is not very distant. But for you, with such advantages and such aims, it is infinitely harder that you are unhappy. My late visit has convinced me too well that this is the case with you: would that the remedy were equally plain! No, my dearest friend, you are not happy: indeed how could you be so? What communion has light with darkness; or you with the inane people your lot is cast among? You are encircled with drivelling and folly;

nothing that your mind can relish or care for; companionless, tho' your heart is full of warm affections: you have sacrificed all for the sake of your improvement, yet you are obstructed almost stopped in your progress towards it. My dearest Jane!

(*Letters*, II, 491-492)

Composition: [December, 1823?].

Manuscript: Yale University.

First Publication: Froude (1882), I, 140.

Texts Consulted: MS; Froude; *Love Letters*, II, 353-354.

Copy-text: MS.

Textual Notes: The undated Yale manuscript is the only surviving text in Carlyle's handwriting, but both Foude and Alexander Carlyle seem to have printed their texts from different manuscripts. Froude's version omits the final stanza, and the poem is titled "To Miss Jane B. Welsh" in *Love Letters*. "For Jane Welsh" is written in Carlyle's hand on the outside of the manuscript.

Emendations:

8	Heaven's] Froude, *Love Letters*; Heavens
29	knell,] Froude, *Love Letters*; knell
38	[Jane]] *Love Letters*; —

Variants:

1	one] One (*Love Letters*)
2	glory's] Glory's (Froude)
4	Sun] sun (Froude)
5	flaming?] flaming. (Froude)
11	thine *were*] '*twere* thine (*Love Letters*); 'twas thine (Froude)
13	*be*] be (Froude)
15	scorning.] scorning! (*Love Letters*)
16	maid!] maid, (Froude)
16	thy gen'rous destiny] as oft thy fate (*Love Letters*): thy destiny as (Froude)
18	Earth's elected] earth's chosen (Froude)
21	fame's] Fame's (Froude)
23	seek;] seek! (*Love Letters*)
27	thee!] thee, (Froude)
30	me!] me. (Froude)
34	life's] Life's (Froude)
38	Heav'n] heaven (*Love Letters*)

7
[Now Fare Thee Well Old Twenty-Three!]

Commentary: This poem was written in Carlyle's journal as he reflect-
ed on his life at the turning of the year. He was twenty-eight
years old, residing with the Bullers at Kinnaird House, working
on *Schiller* and *Wilhelm Meister*, courting Jane, and still suffering
from dyspepsia. A characteristic passage from the journal entry
that accompanies the poem gives an indication of Carlyle's mood:
> Another hour and 1823 is with the years beyond the flood.
> What have I done to mark the course of it? Suffered the
> pangs of Tophet almost daily, grown sicker and sicker,
> alienated by my misery certain of my friends, and worn out
> from my own mind a few remaining capabilities of enjoy-
> ment, reduced my world a *little* nearer the condition of a
> bare haggard desart, where peace and rest for me is none.
> Hopeful youth Mr. C.! Another year or two and it will
> do; another year or two and thou wilt *wholly* be the *caput
> mortum* of thy former self, a creature ignorant, stupid,
> peevish, disappointed, broken-hearted; the veriest wretch
> upon the surface of the globe.
> (*Two Note Books,* pp. 55-56)

Still, all was not gall,, and Carlyle also writes that he has yet a
"glimmering of hope," love of and for his family and other friends,
and "better hopes of *Meister* than I had; tho' still they are very
faint" (*Two Note Books,* p. 56 and pp. 58-59, respectively).

Composition: 31 December, 1823.

Manuscript: Private hands.

First Publication: Froude (1882), I, 162.

Texts Consulted: Froude; *Two Note Books.*

Copy-text: *Two Note Books,* pp. 59-60.

Textual Notes: The only manuscript of the poem is in Carlyle's journal
and is therefore not presently available to scholars. As Norton
is generally judged to have been a more careful editor than was
Froude, Norton's printing has been followed, and Froude's sub-
stantive variants are listed below.

Variants:

    1   three!] three, (Froude)
    2   power] powers

2	art] arts
3	away—Eternity!] away, [∧]
4	*never*] never
6	bringer] bringest
6	grief!] grief;
7	sore] sour
8	The patient heart] The heart

8
[Where Shall I Find Thee]

Commentary: As G. B. Tennyson notes, the only dating for this poem is a note by J. A. S. Barrett that assigns it to the period 1823-1825; but Tennyson also observes that if one takes the phrase "lost and loved ones" literally, then a later date must be assigned since Carlyle's sister Margaret died in 1830, and his father in 1832 ("Poetry," p. 175). Since conclusive evidence is lacking, however, Tennyson's final decision is to abide with the Barrett dating, and that dating is followed in this edition as well.

Composition: [1823-1825?]

Manuscript: Yale University.

First Publication: Tennyson, "Poetry," pp. 175-176.

Texts Consulted: MS; Tennyson.

Copy-text: MS.

Textual Notes: The untitled Yale manuscript provides the only text of the poem, which Tennyson first published in 1963. At the end of the poem Carlyle writes "—Blarney—[.]"

Variants:

12	Peace! There shall I find thee?] In the manuscript the line originally read, "There perhaps I find thee?" but "perhaps" is cancelled, and "shall" is written in above the cancellation; "Peace!" is added before the line in the left margin.

9
To Jane B. Welsh

Commentary: "To Jane B. Welsh" was written at the conclusion of her visit with Carlyle and his family at Hoddam Hill from 2 to 19 September, 1825 (*Love Letters*, II, 354n.). The visit had the air of a traditional engagement visit designed for Carlyle's parents and Jane to meet each other, and from this point on the eventual marriage seemed a certainty. (For Carlyle's recollection of the occasion see his notes on Jane's letter of 2 September in *Letters*, III, 375-380).

Composition: 19 September, 1825.

Manuscript: University of California, Santa Cruz

First Publication: *Love Letters*, II, 354-355.

Texts Consulted: *Love Letters*.

Copy-text: MS.

Textual Notes: *Love Letters* is the only previous printing of the poem.   The manuscript was sold at auction in 1932 and is described in Sotheby's catalogue as "Poem in three stanzas 'To Jane B. Welsh,' 19 *Sept.* 1825, on embossed card . . ." (p. 25).

10

Thunder-Storm [I]

Commentary: Dyer is the authority for attributing this and the following similarly-titled poem to Carlyle (p. 257). Both poems were published in the *Dumfries Monthly Magazine and Literary Compendium*, a local periodical that ran from July, 1825, to December, 1826.   No mention of the poems or of the *Dumfries Monthly Magazine* has yet been discovered among Carlyle materials, but he did contribute to other local periodicals, and it is not implausible that he contributed these poems as well. The *Dumfries Monthly Magazine* at any rate knew something of Carlyle, for the May, 1926, issue carries a brief criticism of the style of "Mr Carlyle, the translator of Wilhelm Meister, and author of the Life of Schlegel [sic]."[1]

Composition: By December, 1825.

Manuscript: Untraced.

First Publication: *Dumfries Monthly Magazine and Literary Compendium*, I (December, 1825), 507-508.

Texts Consulted: *Dumfries Monthly Magazine*.

Copy-Text: *Dumfries Monthly Magazine*.

Textual Notes: *Dumfries Monthly Magazine* provides the only text of the poem; it is dated "December, 1825" on the signature line and initialed "T. C."

Citation:

[1]Vol. II, 419. Part of the criticism of Carlyle's style is this: "He has, perhaps, greater command over the English langauge, and can mould it more successfully to every purpose of composition, than any author of the present day. It can only be said in his disfavour, that he occasionally *commits peculiarities of style*."

11

Thunder-Storm [II]

Commentary: See notes for preceding poem.

Composition: By February, 1826.

Manuscript: Untraced.

First Publication: *Dumfries Monthly Magazine and Literary Compendium*, II (February, 1826), 136.

Texts Consulted: *Dumfries Monthly Magazine.*

Copy-Text: *Dumfries Monthly Magazine.*

Glosses:

41   *Bruit*: 'rumor.'

42   *Sooth*: This may be a misprint for *soothe,* but a meaning for *sooth* in Scots' dialect is 'to make one believe; to impose upon by flattery.' Another possibility is that Carlyle is playing on the received meaning of *sooth* as 'truth' and giving it a verb form.

Textual Notes: *Dumfries Monthly Magazine* provides the only text of the poem; no date is given, but the poem is initialed "T. C."

12

The Sower's Song

Commentary: "The Sower's Song" continues the nature theme. Carlyle sent a copy of the poem to Jane with a letter of 20 March, 1826, wherein he writes, "To rejoice your heart still farther, I send you a small *Sowing Song,* which I manufactured the other night, when too sick and dull to commence the *Life of Goethe*" (*Letters*, IV, 62-63). In a letter to his brother John on the same day, he claims to have composed the poem "one *billus* night and morning, when I could not begin Goethe" (*Letters*, IV, 65).

Composition: [March, 1826].

Manuscript: Yale University.

First Publication: *Chaos*, I, No. 37 [1830], 145-146.

Texts Consulted: MS; *Chaos*; *Fraser's*, III, No. 15 (April, 1831), 390; *Essays*, 2nd ed. (1840), III, 268; *Essays*, People's Edition (1872), VI (Vol. I of *Critical and Micscellaneous Essays*), 290-291.

Copy-text: *Essays*, 2nd ed.

Textual Notes: The Yale manuscript is the only surviving autograph copy of the poem, and the editors of the *Letters* judge it to have been the copy that Carlyle made for Jane and sent with his letter of 20 March, 1826 (*Letters*, IV, 62n.). The title is underlined twice in the manuscript, and the manuscript exhibits both early and later wordings of the poem, with the revisions appearing to have been written in a different ink and perhaps with a different pen. The manuscript is dated "March, 1826." The printing in *Chaos* is also dated "March 1826" and is signed "J. Ce." The printings in the 2nd ed. of the *Essays* and in the People's Edition are identical.

Variants:

1   hands to seedsheet, boys] In the manuscript these words are written above the words "yarely and soft, my boys"; *Chaos* and *Fraser's* both print "yarely and soft, my boys[.]"

2   We step and we cast; old Time's on wing] In the manuscript the original line reads, "Come step we, and cast; for Time's o'wing"; "We" is written above "Come[,]" "and" above "we," "we" above "and[,]" "old" above "for[,]" and "on" above "o'"; *Chaos* and *Fraser's* both print the original "Come step we, and cast; for Time's o'wing[.]"

3   And would ye] And wouldst thou (MS, *Chaos, Fraser's*)

5-8]   These lines are not underlined in the manuscript nor italicized in *Chaos* or *Fraser's*. The same is true for the other refrain lines in the poem.

7   so] so, (*Chaos*)

9   is a pleasure to see] has put on, you see, (MS, *Chaos, Fraser's*)

10   In sunshiny cloak] Her sunshiny cloak (MS, *Chaos*); Her
     sunshiny coat (*Fraser's*)
11   Year] year (MS, *Chaos, Fraser's*)
12   Years] years (MS, *Chaos, Fraser's*)
15   Six Thousand] six thousand (MS, *Chaos, Fraser's*)
19   steady and sure] lightly and soft (MS, *Chaos, Fraser's*)
20   we] let's (MS, *Chaos, Fraser's*)

13
Cui Bono

Commentary: "Cui Bono" probably dates from late 1826. An early
    version of the poem was printed in *Chaos*, where it is dated 1826
    and signed "J. C."; also, Heinrich Kraeger pointed out that the
    poem was intended to be included in "Wotton Reinfred," Car-
    lyle's unfinished novel that he began in Edinburgh in the spring
    of 1827.[1]   Carlyle quoted the second stanza of the poem in a
    letter to his mother on 11 August, 1827, and in the letter he
    writes,

> This life is but a series of meetings and partings; and many
> a tear one might shed while these "few and evil days" pass
> over us: but we hope there is another scene, to which this
> is but the passage, where good and holy affections shall live
> as in their home, and for true friends there shall be no more
> partings appointed. God grant we may all have our lot made
> sure in that earnest and enduring country! For surely this
> world the more one thinks of it seems the more fluctuating,
> hollow and unstable: what are its proudest hopes but bubbles
> on the stream of Time, which the next rushing wave will
> scatter into air. (*Letters*, IV, 243)

Composition: [Late?] 1826.
Manuscript: National Library of Scotland MS 519.52. (letter to
    Carlyle's mother, containing stanza two and dated 11 August,
    1827; printed in *Letters*, IV, 243).
First Publication: *Chaos*, I, No. 28 [1830], 110.
Texts Consulted: MS; *Chaos*; *Fraser's* II, No. 18 (September, 1830),
    178; *Original Reviews*; *Essays*, 2nd ed. (1840), III, 264; *Essays*,
    People's Edition (1872), VI, (Vol. I of *Critical and Miscellaneous
    Essays*), 288-289; Froude (1882), II, 420-421.

Copy-text: *Essays,* 2nd ed.

Gloss:

> *Cui Bono*: Literally 'to whom for a good,' but usually translated 'What good will it do?' 'Who will be the better for it?'

Textual Notes: The only manuscript portion of "Cui Bono" is that included in the 11 August,1827, letter to Carlyle's mother. The *Chaos* text seems to represent the earliest state of the poem, certainly the earliest printed version, with the *Fraser's* text standing as an intermediate version between that in *Chaos* and the final version in *Essays.* The poem was sent to *Fraser's,* together with other pieces, on 6 August, 1830 (*Letters,* V, 127). The text in *Original Reviews* is an unrevised clipping from *Fraser's.* The printings in 2nd ed. and People's Edition of *Essays* are identical. Even though Froude's text exhibits ten variants in accidentals, since he indicated that he was printing the text from the *Essays* and not from some now-lost manuscript, his variants are not listed below.

Variants:

Cui Bono] untitled in *Chaos*; Cui Bono? (*Fraser's*)

1 smiling] golden (*Chaos*)

4 urchin] Urchin (*Chaos*)

5 Life] life (MS)

6 shore;-] shore (MS)

10 Vainly strives, and fights, and frets] Fighting fierce for hollow nuts (*Chaos, Fraser's*)

Citation:

[1] "Carlyles Stellung zur Deutschen Sprach und Literatur," *Anglia,* 22 (1899), 332. The poem is not actually quoted in "Wotton," nor is it mentioned by title; but the line "What is Hope? A golden rainbow, etc." is inserted at the point where one of the songs begins (in *Last Words of Thomas Carlyle* [1892; rpt. West Germany: Gregg International, 1971], p. 90).

14

[The Hildebrands]

Commentary: This poem appears in Carlyle's journal between the entries dated 16 January, 1827, and March, 1827.

Composition: January-March, 1827.
Manuscript: Private hands.
First Publication: *Two Note Books* (1898), p. 103.
Texts Consulted: *Two Note Books*.
Copy-text: *Two Note Books*.
Glosses:

> *Hildebrands*: Hildebrand became Pope Gregory VII (1073-1085) and is noted for having carried out church reforms and for having attempted to subordinate secular rulers to papal authority. Although his enemies tried to picture him as an evil and grasping genius, he was canonized in 1584.

> *Borgias*: The Borgias were the Italian Renaissance family often cited as prototypes of cunning and unscrupulous rulers. Cesare (c. 1475-1507) is probably the best known member of the family, having served as the model that Machiavelli idealized in *The Prince* (1513), but Cesare's sister Lucrezia (1480-1519) is also associated with dark intrigue in the popular imagination.

Textual Notes: Since the poem appears in Carlyle's journal, the manuscript is not presently available to scholars. The printing in *Two Note Books* provides the only text of the poem.

Emendation:

> 4   wage] printed by itself on a separate line following

15
[Scotland Prides]

Commentary: Carlyle's correspondence with Goethe began when Carlyle sent Goethe a copy of his translation of *Wilhelm Meister* in June, 1824, and Goethe responded with a letter in October; from then on an exchange of letters and gifts continued until Goethe's death in 1832. "Scotland Prides" was written to accompany a highland bonnet that Jane made for Ottilie von Goethe and included in a package that was sent to Weimar on 22 December, 1829 (*Letters*, V, 38n., 48). As G. B. Tennyson notes, positive identification of the authorship of the occasional poems that were sent to Weimar may no longer be possible ("Poetry," p. 163n.). However, one should note that in a letter to Carlyle's mother written about 15 December, 1829, Jane mentions the package to Goethe and writes, "there is also a smart Highland bonnet for his daughter-in-law—accompanied by a nice little verse of poetry professing to be written by me but in truth I did not write a word of it . . ."; she then quotes "Scotland Prides" (*Letters,* V, 39). Nevertheless, this poem and several of the other poems that went to Weimar have sometimes been attributed to Jane, and the reason is clear: they were all in her handwriting, and many of them (including "Scotland Prides") were signed by her as well. But, in this context two things must be kept sight of. For one thing, the manuscripts that survive in Weimar bear testimony as to why they were written out by Jane — because they all exhibit her best and most ornamental calligraphy, not her usual hand. No extant manuscript of Thomas Carlyle's shows a comparable degree of "fancy penmanship," and this fact must explain why even his known poems seem to have been transcribed by Jane before they were sent to Weimar. Secondly, Jane was apparently in the habit of signing her own name to Carlyle's poems. For example, Helen Welsh's autograph book at Yale contains a copy of "Cui Bono" that is in Jane's handwriting and is signed "J C," and the printed versions of "Cui Bono," "Tragedy of the Night-Moth," and "The Sower's Song" in *Chaos* all bear her initials as well.[1]

Composition: December, 1829.

Manuscript: Goethe-Schiller Archiv, Weimar, MS II, 5,6; National Library of Scotland MS 601.16 (Jane's letter to Carlyle's mother, 15 December, 1829; printed in *Letters,* V, 39).

First Publication: Froude (1882), II, 102.

Texts Consulted: Goethe-Schiller Archiv MS; National Library of Scotland MS; Froude; *Correspondence Between Goethe and Carlyle* (1887), p. 157.

Copy-text: Goethe-Schiller Arvhiv MS.

Textual Notes: The Weimar manuscript is signed "Jane W. B. Carlyle" and dated "Craigenputtoch 15th December 1829[.]" *Correspondence Between Goethe and Carlyle* prints the text of the Weimar manuscript with slight variations in accidentals, and Froude prints the text from the letter now at the National Library of Scotland, also with slight variations in accidentals and with one substantive variant, probably arising from an oversight.

Variants:

1   "Bonnet Blue,"] "bonnet blue", (NLS MS)
2   Love or War] love or war (NLS MS)
3]   no punctuation (NLS MS)
4   Of my Scottish Love] love, (NLS MS); Of Scottish love (Froude)
4   !] . (NLS MS)

Citation:

[1] Alexander Carlyle reported that the manuscript of "To a Swallow Building under Our Eaves" was also in Jane Carlyle's handwriting (*Love Letters*, II, 359-360n.), and the manuscript of "Today" that is kept at the National Library of Scotland is also in her handwriting, but it is signed by Carlyle. Also see her letter of 11 November, 1822, to Carlyle where she writes, "I inserted some of your verses (without your name) in the Album of one of my acquaintances, and I understand they are figuring in the albums of all the little Ladies and right honourables in the county. Are you angry? I assure you no one knows by whom they are written" (*Letters*, II, 198-199). She did not sign everything that went to Weimar, though, for the poem beginning "All Mute and dim" is not signed; and although the manuscript is in Jane's best formal handwriting, the poem has always been attributed to Carlyle.

16
[To the Poet]

Commentary: Also included in the package that was sent to Goethe on 22 December, 1829, was a lock of Jane's hair and an accompanying poem (*Letters*, V, 38n., 48; also see the note to the preceding poem in this edition). The poem had the distinction of having been mistaken for one of Goethe's own after his death and was first published in the Weimar Edition of his works.[1]

Composition: December, 1829.
Manuscript: Goethe-Schiller Archiv, Weimar, MS, 236.
First Publication: Weimar Edition of Goethe's *Works*, V, 78.
Texts Consulted: MS; Weimar Edition.
Copy-text: MS.
Textual Notes: The Weimar manuscript is the only existing Carlyle

family manuscript of the poem, and all previous printings of the poem are of that manuscript. The lock of Jane's hair is still kept at Weimar with the manuscript, and the manuscript is written in her best hand, signed "Jane W. B. Carlyle[,]" dated "Craigenputtoch, 15 December 1829[,]" and addressed "To the Poet in Return Gift for Gift."

Citation:

[1]Leonard L. Mackall, "Verse von Frau Carlyle unter Goethes Gedichten an Personen," *Goethe Jahrbuch,* 25 (1904), 234-236. Mackall writes that the error occurred because Goethe had transcribed the poem in his own hand, apparently with the intent to have it printed in *Chaos.* The transcription was later found among the *Chaos* papers, and, owing to the fact that the original editors of the Weimar Edition had died, the poem was assumed to have been Goethe's and was printed as such. Mackall also notes that Alexander Carlyle had written him a private letter in which he expressed the opinion that Jane had not written poetry, but had only copied poems from her husband and mother (p. 234n.). The manuscript of this letter is in the Johns Hopkins University Library and says, "I hardly think Mrs Carlyle ever wrote a Verse of Poetry herself: what has been attributed to her, by Froude and others, was written either by Carlyle or by Mrs Welsh (who had a decided talent for rhyming) and merely *copied* by Mrs Carlyle." Also see Alexander Carlyle's note on this poem in *Love Letters,* where he attributes it to Carlyle (I, 94-95n.).

17

My Own Four Walls

Commentary: The poem dates from the period, 1828-1830, but the desire for a place of his own was nothing new to Carlyle. For instance, during his first visit to London in 1824 he writes to his brother John in November, "My schemes are various, and as yet mostly vague. Almost all of them involve *being in a house of my own,* somewhere in the country, within reach of London or Edinburgh; I rather think of the latter. The means for keeping up that projected household are next to be devised" (*Letters,* III, 209). His "schemes" were first realized when his father leased

Hoddam Hill farm for him, and he and other members of his family moved there in May, 1825. As part of an explanation to Jane of why her mother should not live with them after their marriage, he describes something of his life at Hoddam Hill in a letter of 2 April, 1826:

> It is inexpressible what an increase of happiness, and of consciousness, wholesome consciousness of inward dignity I have gained since I came within the walls of this poor cottage. My own four walls! For in my state this primeval law of Nature [that the man should rule in the house and not the woman] acts on *me* with double and triple force. And how cheaply it is purchased, and how smoothly managed! They simply admit that I am *Herr im Hause* ["master of the house"; *Letters* translation], and act on this conviction. Here is no grumbling about my habitudes and whims: if I choose to dine on fire and brimstone, they will cook it for me to their best skill; thinking only that I am an unintelligible mortal; perhaps in their secret souls, a kind of humourist, *facheuse* ["troublesome"; *Letters* translation] to deal with, but no bad soul after all, and *not* to be dealt with in *any* other way. My own four walls!
> (*Letters*, IV, 69-70)

The "Four Walls of the poem, though, are surely at Craigenputtoch. Alexander Carlyle notes that Carlyle often called Craigenputtoch the "Whinstone House" or the "Moorland House" and further observes that since the Carlyles moved to Craigenputtoch in May, 1828, and George IV died in January, 1830, the date of the poem must lie somewhere between those two dates; he suggests autumn of 1829 (*Love Letters*, II, 356n.).

Composition: [May, 1828-January, 1830?].

Manuscript: Yale University.

First Publication: Froude (1882), I, 324-325.

Texts Consulted: MS; Froude; *Love Letters*, II, 355-356; Miller, pp. 253-254.

Copy-text: MS.

Textual Notes: The Yale manuscript is the only one whose location is known. The title is underlined twice in the manuscript, and for composition A. Carlyle suggests "About 1830" in a note written the lower left corner of the manuscript. Alexander Carlyle's text in *Love Letters* seems to reflect a different, now-lost manuscript version, and Frank Miller's printing is from an untraced manuscript copy taken down from Carlyle's dictation by Archibald Glen when he visited Carlyle at Craigenputtoch in 1834 (Miller, p. 253). Froude's printing, except for accidentals, seems to represent the text of the Yale manuscript.

Emendations:

1   are] *Love Letters,* Miller; is
25   be,] Froude, *Love Letters,* Miller; be

Variants:

3   As fast, on willing Nag, I haste,] As fast on willing nag I haste (Froude, Miller); As fast, on willing nag, I haste (*Love Letters*)

5   tossing] "Storm-tost" is cancelled in the manuscript, and "tossing" is written above it.

5   Black, tossing clouds, with scarce a glimmer,] No punctuation (Froude, Miller); Black tossing clouds, with dim light-glimmers, (*Love Letters*)

6   Envelope] What looks like "Even" is cancelled before "Envelope [.]"

6   Earth,] earth (Froude); Earth (Miller)

7   wifekin watches, coffee-pot doth simmer,] Wifekin waits and coffee simmers (*Love Letters*); Wife-kin (Miller)

8   walls!] walls. (Froude, Miller)

9   befals!] befals; (Froude, Miller)

14   their] This word is written over what appears to have originally been "his" in the manuscript.

14   their] those (Froude); his (*Love Letters*)

15   abide] The original "'bide" is cancelled before this word in the manuscript.

18   Friend's] friends' (Froude, Miller); Friends' (*Love Letters*)

18   Monarch's,] monarchs', (Froude); Monarch's (*Love Letters*); monarchs' (Miller)

19   Castle] castle (Froude, *Love Letters,* Miller)

21   Knaves] knaves (Froude, *Love Letters,* Miller)

21   do] The word is written above the line between "Knaves" and "make" in the manuscript.

21   a] This is written above a cancelled "any" in the manuscript.

21   do make a rout] make any rout (Miller)

25   The] A (Miller)
27   Books] books (Froude, Miller)

18
The Sigh

Commentary: Froude claims that this poem is ample evidence of
Carlyle's "occasional tenderness" and that it is too bad it was
not "formed into habit" insofar as Jane was concerned (Froude,
II, 341).   The poem embodies the essence, both good and bad,
of the struggles of the Craigenputtoch years.

Composition: January, 1830.

Manuscript: Yale University.

First Publication: Froude (1882), II, 421-422.

Texts Consulted: MS; Froude.

Copy-text: MS.

Textual Notes: The Yale manuscript is the only one that survives, and
it is dated "29th January, 1830[.]" The title is underlined twice
in the manuscript. Froude prints the Yale manuscript with many
variants in accidentals, some owing to genuine ambiguity in the
manuscript with respect to capitalization, and his variants for
ambiguous letters are listed below.

Variants:

1   Wife] wife (Froude)
13   Sky] What looks to have been originally "Skys" is cancelled
preceding this word in the manuscript.
15   Universe] universe
16   maker] Maker
17   done] An original "o'er" is cancelled preceding this word
in the manuscript.
18   wondrous] This word is written above a cancelled "stranger"
in the manuscript.
19   Loved] loved
24   look'd] This word is written above a cancelled "hop'd" in the
manuscript.

19
[O Time]

Commentary: This poem is from Carlyle's journal, where on the
preceding pages he meditates on several of the themes that found
their way into *Sartor Resartus,* and then he also asks,

> What is Poetry? Do I really love Poetry? I sometimes
> fancy almost, not. The jingle of maudlin persons, with
> their mere (even genuine) "sensibility" is unspeakably
> fatiguing to me. My greatly most delightful reading is,
> where some Goethe musically *teaches* me. Nay, *any* fact,
> relating especially to man, is still valuable and pleasing.
> (*Two Note Books,* p. 151)

Later in the same passage, and very shortly before the poem, he
voices the characteristic theme that the poem echoes:

> Doubtful it is in the highest degree, whether ever I shall
> make men hear my voice to any purpose or not. Certain
> only that I shall be a *failure* if I do not, and unhappy: nay
> unhappy enough (that is with suffering enough) even if I do.
> My own talent I cannot in the remotest attempt at estimat-
> ing. Something superior often does seem to be in me, and
> hitherto the world has been very kind; but *many* things
> inferior also; so that I can strike no balance. —Hang it,
> *try*; and leave this *Grübeln!* ["speculating"; Norton's trans-
> lation.]
>
> *What we have done* is the only mirror that can show us
> what we *are.* (*Two Notes Books,* p. 152)

Composition: March-April, 1830.

Manuscript: Private hands.

First Publication: Froude (1882), II, 82.

Texts Consulted: Froude; *Two Note Books,* p. 152.

Copy-text: *Two Note Books.*

Textual Notes: Since the poem is written in Carlyle's journal, the
manuscript is not presently available to scholars. The text that
Norton prints in *Two Note Books* comes between the entries
dated "March" and 12 April [1830]. Froude of course also
had access to the journal, so his single substantive variant is listed
below.

Variant:

4   getting!] getting. (Froude)

20
[Thy Quiet Goodness]

Commentary: Carlyle's sister Margaret died in Dumfries (where she had been taken for medical care) on 22 June, 1830, at age twenty-seven.[1] She had been the favorite daughter, and her death was the first break in the family, and a loss that Carlyle continued to recall in sadness over thirty years later. Carlyle was in charge of the funeral arrangements for Margaret's burial in Ecclefechan, and in a long letter of 29 June to his brother John he sends a detailed account of his sister's last days and of the funeral, and he includes this description of Margaret's character:

> I have often thought, she had attained all in Life that Life could give her: a just, true, meekly invincible, completed character; which I, and so many others, by far more ambitious paths seek for in vain. She was, in some points, I may say deliberately, superior to any woman I have ever seen: her simple clearness of head and heart, her perfect fairness, and quiet, unpretending, brief decisiveness, in thought, word and act, for in all these she was remarkable, made up so true and brave a spirit as, in that unaffected guise, we shall hardly look upon again. She might have been wife to a Scottish Martyr, and spoken stern truths to the ear of Tyrants, had she been called to that work: as it is, she sleeps in a pure grave; and our peasant maiden, to us who knew her, is more than King's daughters. Let us forever remember her, and love her; but cease from henceforth to mourn for her. (*Letters,* V, 118)

On 14 July Carlyle again writes to John, and in the letter he includes the poem which he had first composed in his journal. In the letter the poem follows these lines: "We are all sad and dull about her that is laid in the Earth: I dream of her almost nightly, and feel not indeed sorrow, for what is Life but a continual Dying? —yet a strange obstruction, and haunting remembrance. Let us banish all this; for it is profitless and foolish . . ." (*Letters,* V, 121).

Composition: 30 June, 1830.

Manuscript: National Library of Scotland MS 522.84 (letter to John Carlyle, 14 July, 1830; printed in *Letters,* V, 120-123).

First Publication: Froude (1882), II, 112.

Texts Consulted: MS; Froude; *Two Note Books*, p. 157.

Copy-text: National Library of Scotland MS.

Textual Notes: The earliest version of the poem is that from the journal entry for 30 June, 1830, and the manuscript is therefore not available to scholars; however, Norton describes the manuscript revisions in his printing in *Two Note Books,* and his details are given below. The version that Carlyle included in his letter of 14 July represents a further revision of the poem, and it was the text from the letter that Froude printed.

Variants:

1   spirit] Norton reports that this word replaced an erased "heart so" in the manuscript, and he prints the word above the line over the erasure.

2]   Norton prints the line as having originally read, "With tears what boots it here to tell?" "With tears" was then erased, and "now with tears" was added above the title to replace the also erased "here[.]"

3   Rest] Norton shows two changes here: the original word was "God[,]" which was erased, and "Rest" was written above the erased word; then "Rest" was itself erased and replaced by "Peace" written above the line and immediately preceding the erased "Rest[.]"

3   lies] is

4   Loved Sister,] Thou loved one,

4   take our long] Norton shows an uncancelled "for a while," here with "take our long" written directly above it.

Citation:

[1] Some doubt exists as to the cause of Margaret's death: nineteenth-century writers attributed it to consumption, but John Clubbe writes that it was probably cancer (*Froude's Life of Carlyle,* abridged and edited by John Clubbe [Columbus, Ohio: Ohio State University Press, 1979], p. 665, n. 21).

21

The Wandering Spirits

Commentary: In his journal entries of between 7 and 9 September,

1830, Carlyle writes, *"Nulla dies sine linea!* ["no day without a line"]—Eheu! Eheu! ["alas! alas!] Yesterday (Monday) accordingly I wrote a thing in dactyls, entitled the *Wandering Spirits,* which now fills and then filled me 'with detestation and abhorrence.' No matter: to day I must do the like. *Nulla dies sine linea!* To the persevering, they say, all things are possible. Possible or impossible, I have no other implement for trying" (*Two Note Books,* pp. 167-168). As G. B. Tennyson notes, this is Carlyle's only attempt at poetic dialogue, and Tennyson feels that the poem seems to be indebted to the confrontation of Faust and the *Erdegeist* in Goethe's *Faust* ("Poetry," p. 176).

Composition: 7 September, 1830.

Manuscript: Yale University (watermark 1827).

First Publication: Tennyson, "Poetry," pp. 176-178.

Texts Consulted: MS; Tennyson.

Copy-text: MS.

Textual Notes: The Yale manuscript provides the only authoritative text of the poem, but Carlyle made several revisions on the manuscript, some of which make his final intentions ambiguous. Following the poem Carlyle wrote on the manuscript, "Trash, Trash, the Penny-writer!—September 7th 1830—The measure not worth correcting."

Emendations:

12-13] In the manuscript these lines are in reverse order, but Carlyle numbered them 1 and 2 respectively (by line numbers in this edition) in the margin. Since a change of speakers does not seem appropriate here, Carlyle's numbering is interpreted to indicate that the order of the lines should be reversed.

15   awoke] "Awoke" is the reading in the manuscript, but "Chaos" was added in front of what was the original opening word.

39] God.] God

Variants:

3] What looks to have been "to" or "be" is cancelled following "Here" in the manuscript.

10   come] In the manuscript "then" is cancelled following "come,"; the comma should also obviously be regarded as belonging to the cancelled word.

11]   "From" is cancelled following "Of" in the manuscript.

14]   In the manuscript "chaos" following "that" is cancelled.

15   Chaos] This word is added before "Awoke" in the manuscript.

15]   "I have" is cancelled following "space" in the manuscript.

16]   "I have" is added before "Figure" in the manuscript.

25]   In the manuscript "must" following "I" is cancelled. Tennyson prints "I must wear[.]"

26]   What looks like "me" or "my" is cancelled following "command" in the manuscript.

26]   "Pain" is cancelled following "and" in the manuscript.

28   compassd] Originally the word was "Encompassd" in the manuscript; the *En* is cancelled.

32]   "He" is cancelled following "lone" in the manuscript.

38]   In the manuscript "our" following "For" is cancelled.

39]   In the manuscript "is our Guidance" following "God" is cancelled.

40]   "And perhaps" is cancelled before "And who knows" in the manuscript.

41]   "D" is cancelled following "But" in the manuscript.

22
The Beetle

Commentary: On Thursday, 9 September, 1830, Carlyle writes in his journal, "Wrote a fractionlet of verse entitled THE BEETLE (a real incident on Glaisters Moor [at Craigenputtoch]), which alas! must stand for the *Linea* both of Tuesday and Wednesday. To day I am to try I know not what. Greater clearness will arrive; I make far most progress when I *walk*, on solitary roads—of which there are enough here" (*Two Note Books*, p. 170).

Composition: 8 September, 1830.

Manuscript: Berg Collection of the New York Public Library.

First Publication: *Fraser's Magazine*, III, No. 13 (February, 1831), 72.

Texts Consulted: MS; *Fraser's*; *Original Reviews*; *Essays*, 2nd ed. (1840), III, 270-271; *Essays*, People's Edition (1872), VI, (Vol. I of *Critical and Miscellaneous Essays*), 292.

Copy-text: *Essays*, 2nd ed.

Glosses:

- 10   *cark*: 'burden of responsibility,' 'That which burdens the spirit.'
- 10   *moil*: 'toil,' 'drudgery.'
- 17   *skaith*: variant of *scathe*; 'harm' 'injury.'
- 23   *Bel*: Babylonian form of *Baal.*

Textual Notes: The Berg Collection's manuscript is the only surviving manuscript of the poem and is dated "8th September 1830." The manuscript version of the poem is the earliest and contains substantive variants; all printed versions of the poem exhibit i-dentical substantive revisions as the *Essays*, 2nd ed. text and con-tain only slight accidental variants. The *Original Reviews* volume contains a clipping of the *Fraser's* printing.

Variants:

- 8   head of house] Head of House (MS)
- 17   Alas,] Alas (MS)
- 22   wonders] marvels (MS)
- 24   chief of wonders] In the manuscript the original wording here was "wondrous lights of"; the phrase was cancelled, and "chief of wonders" was written beneath it.
- 25   'ancient family,'] ancient family, (MS)
- 27   What] No (MS)
- 27   ?] . (MS)
- 28]   Good Lord, *thy* Ancestor was in Noah's Ark. (MS)

23

Absent

Commentary: Alexander Carlyle believed "Absent" to have been written to Jane sometime during the Craigenputtoch period, pos-sibly after Carlyle had returned from a visit to his mother at Scotsbrig; on the basis of the paper and the handwriting he sug-gests 1831 as the likely year for composition (*Love Letters*, II, 356-357n.).

Composition: [1831?].

Manuscript: Yale University (watermark 1827).

First Publication: *Love Letters* (1909), II, 356.

Texts Consulted: MS; *Love Letters.*

Copy-text: MS.

Gloss:

> [1]*Rose*: Wilson notes that Jane Carlyle loved roses and grew them at Craigenputtoch (*Mr. Froude and Carlyle* [New York: Dodd, Mead, 1898], p. 115).

Textual Notes: The Yale manuscript is the only one that survives, but since Alexander Carlyle prints one difference in wording, it is not inconceivable that he used a different manuscript that is now lost. The title is underlined twice in the manuscript.

Variants:

> 9   ever] aye (*Love Letters*)
>
> 18   one] One

24
For the Poet

Commentary: This poem was sent to Goethe for the occasion of his eightieth birthday (28 August, 1831), either with Carlyle's letter of 10 June (after a delay in mailing) or with the package containing the seal that Carlyle had collected a subscription for and sent as a birthday gift around 5 July (*Letters*, V, 290n.). Goethe recorded receipt of the package in his journal on 18 August, and in a letter to Carlyle of 19 August he mentions the silhouettes that were sent in the same package.[1] It seems likely, therefore, that the poem was included with the birthday package.

Composition: 16 June, 1831.

Manuscript: Goethe-Schiller Archiv, Weimar.

First Publication: Chaos, II, No. 2 [1831], 6.

Texts Consulted: Goethe-Schiller MS; *Chaos*; *Correspondence Between Goethe and Carlyle* (1887), p. 286; *Letters*, V, 290.

Copy-text: MS.

Textual Notes: The only extant manuscript is the Weimar one. This unsigned manuscript is addressed "For the Poet[,]" written in Jane's best handwriting, and dated "Craigenputtoch 16 June 1831[.]" All printings give the text of the Weimar manuscript without changes in wording.

Emendation:

> 4   replies.]   *Correspondence Between Goethe and Carlyle;* replies —

Variants:
1   Shadows] shadows (*Chaos*)
2   Friend] Friends (*Chaos*)
Citation:
[1]Printed in *Letters,* V, 307-308. A silhouette of Jane is still kept
at Weimar, and the stencil for it is at the National Library of
Scotland, where it is catalogued as MS 518.104.

25
[Priest-Ridden]

Commentary: This poem was written in Carlyle's journal between 24
October and 2 November, 1831, while he was in London seeking a
publisher for *Sartor Resartus.* Although the poem strikes a general
Carlylean note, it may include reference to a specific concern.
Alexander Carlyle writes that Jane consulted Carlyle's mother
twice about Jane's "maternal hopes" during the Craigenputtoch
years,[1] and apparently Jane believed those hopes about to be
realized in 1831 since A. Carlyle also reports that "In the summer
of 1831 her sister-in-law Miss Jean Aitken staid with her during
Carlyle's absence in London, and helped her to prepare a tiny
wardrobe for the expected little new-comer." Jane joined Car-
lyle in London on 1 October, but A. Carlyle writes that the hard-
ship of the journey "to London, and in London" induced a weak-
ening of health, and these particular "maternal hopes" ended (*Love
Letters,* I, 319n.).
Composition: [October?] 1831.
Manuscript: Private Hands.
First Publication: *Two Note Books* (1898), p. 216.
Texts Consulted: *Two Note Books.*
Copy-text: *Two Note Books.*
Textual Notes: *Two Note Books* gives the only previous printing of
the poem. The manuscript is in Carlyle's journal and is not pres-
ently available to scholars.
Citation:
[1]Alexander Carlyle and Sir James Crichton-Browne, *The Nemesis
of Froude* (New York and London: John Lane, 1903), p. 72. The
question of whether or not Jane was pregnant remains to be

proved. Alexander Carlyle's claims are disregarded by Lawrence and Elizabeth Hanson, *Necessary Evil: The Life of Jane Welsh Carlyle* (London: Constable, 1952), pp. 549-550, who, based upon certain documents, conclude that she was not. The whole question of the Carlyles' sexual relationship has been hotly contested over the years; for a summary of the arguments, see G. B. Tennyson's bibliographic essay in *Victorian Prose: A Guide to Research,* ed. David J. Delaura (New York: Modern Language Association, 1973), pp. 51-54.

26

[Oh! Life Turmoil]

Commentary: The poem appears in Carlyle's journal between the entries of 11 August and 3 September, 1832, after he had returned in March from London and his unsuccessful attempt to find a publisher for *Sartor Resartus.* His despondent mood is reflected in his journal entry: "Am inclined to consider myself a most sorry knave; but must cease *considering* and begin work . . ." (Froude, II, 249).

Composition: [August?] 1832.

Manuscript: Private hands.

First Publication: Froude (1882), II, 308.

Texts Consulted: Froude.

Copy-text: Froude.

Textual Notes: Froude's is the only previous printing of the poem. The manuscript is in Carlyle's journal and is therefore not presently available to scholars.

27

Drumwhirn Bridge

Commentary: "Drumwhirn Bridge" was first positively identified as Carlyle's by Frank Miller, who writes that the poem was taken down from Carlyle's dictation by Archibald Glen, probably when Glen spent a fortnight at Craigenputtoch in January, 1834.[1] Drumwhirn is in Balmaclellan on the road to Craigenputtoch,

and the river Orr forms part of the west boundary of Craigenput-
toch.

Composition: November, 1832.

Manuscript: Untraced.

First Publication: *Leigh Hunt's London Journal,* I, No. 30 (22 October,
1834), 238.

Texts Consulted: *Leigh Hunt's London Journal*: Wylie, pp. 230-231;
Miller, p. 252.

Copy-text: *Leigh Hunt's London Journal.*

Textual Notes: The title of the poem is misprinted in *Leigh Hunt's
London Journal* to read "Drumwhinn"; the poem is dated "No-
vember, 1832" and is unsigned. Wylie prints his text from *Hunt's.*
Frank Miller states that his text was printed from the manuscript
in Archibald Glen's handwriting that was then (1910) owned by
Glen's daughter Mrs. Graham of Kilbarchan and that was dated
"November 1832" (the date of composition, not of dictation);
the location of this manuscript is not now known. All variants
listed below are from Miller's text.

Emendation:

Drumwhirn] Miller: Drumwhinn

Variants:

1	autumn] Autumn (Miller)
7	Heaven] heaven
11	Vain] Raise
11	bleak] Black
16	earth] Earth
19	tongue] Tongue
21	it] *it*
23	Since] Since,
32	meet] met
33	!] ,
36	*this*] this
37	Bridge] bridge
39	time] Time

Citation:

[1] *The Poets of Dumfriesshire,* p. 252. See also Carlyle's letter of
13 December, 1833, where he gives Glen directions to Craigen-
puttoch (printed in *Letters,* VII, 51).

28

Crichope Linn

Commentary: On 7 September, 1833, Carlyle writes to Jane, who is
visiting Moffat near Templand with her mother and Helen Welsh,
and describes his activities of the past couple of days at Craigen-
puttoch. One of his activities was writing this poem, for in the
letter he included a copy of the poem and writes, "After tea, I
did—what think you? Composed the following beautiful Doggrel
on the Linn of Crichope, and fair Ludovina (I hope, she is fair):
quite a jewel of a piece . . ." (*Letters,* VI, 434). Once a refuge
for the Scottish Covenanters, Crichope Linn was a tourist attrac-
tion in the nineteenth century;[1] it was a waterfall with a narrow
cleft, which Carlyle called "a strange high-lying chasmy place,"[2]
and it was located near Templand.

Composition: 7 September, 1833.

Manuscript: National Library of Scotland MS 610.22 (letter to Jane,
7 September, 1833; printed in *Letters,* VI, 435-436).

First Publication: Froude (1882), II, 366.

Texts Consulted: MS; Froude; John M. Sloan, *The Carlyle Country*
(1904; rpt. New York: Haskell House, 1973), p. 219; *Letters,*
VI, 435-436.

Copy-text: MS.

Gloss:

  Loquitur Genius Loci: 'The guardian spirit of the place speaks.'

Textual Notes: The National Library of Scotland manuscript supplies
the only authoritative text of the poem. Froude prints over a
dozen variants in substantives and accidentals, but since none of
them could have resulted from ambiguity in the manuscript, they
are not listed below. Sloan prints Froude's text.

Emendation:

  10   Still] Froude, *Letters*; still

Variants:

  5-8]   "or omit this?" is written in the left margin beside the
       stanza.

  5   cast] This is written above a cancelled "fast" in the manu-
       script.

  6   Arches, see,] A cancelled "Flood-borne" appears between
       the lines directly above this in the manuscript.

Citations:

[1] According to *The Third Statistical Account of Scotland: The County of Dumfries,* ed. George Houston (Glasgow: William Collins Sons, 1962), Crichope Linn is now overgrown and deserted (p. 217). For a further description of the Linn in Carlyle's time, see John M. Sloan, *The Carlyle Country,* pp. 216-220.

[2] *Reminiscences,* ed. Charles Eliot Norton (London: Macmillan, 1887), I, 169.

29

An Hannchen

Commentary: "An Hannchen" is the little dedicatory poem that Carlyle inscribed on the inside front cover of the *Original Reviews* volume of his essays and reviews that he had specially bound for Jane in 1833.

Composition: November, 1833.

Manuscript: Yale University.

First Publication: Tennyson, "Poetry," p. 175.

Texts Consulted: MS; Tennyson.

Copy-text: MS.

Gloss:

'To Jenny
My Works, too-shabby children
Of hard fate, of wit hacked apart,
Stand called to account before you, like condemned criminals,
Dearest not-too-strict-a judge!'

Textual Notes: The *Original Reviews* volume at Yale is unique and supplies the text of the poem, which was first printed by Tennyson. The title is underlined twice in the manuscript, and the poem is signed "T. C." and dated "November, 1833."

Variant:

4   Richterinn] Richtersinn (Tennyson)

30
Adieu

Commentary: Probably the best dating for "Adieu" and for the following two poems is Carlyle's own of 1823-1833, which he assigned to all of the "Fractions" in *Critical and Miscellaneous Essays*.   D. A. Wilson observes that the poem is not explicitly addressed to anyone and was not given to Jane, and on the basis of that observation he suggests that the poem was written as early as 1822 and is about Margaret Gordon (*Carlyle Till Marriage*, p. 255). G. B. Tennyson admits the possibility of the 1822 date, but points out that since the poem is *not* specifically addressed to anyone, one has no real evidence by which to link it to Margaret Gordon ("Poetry," p. 166).   Certainly no positive evidence has surfaced, but circumstantial evidence may support Wilson's claim.   For instance, one should note that in Margaret Gordon's final letter to Carlyle, wherein she ended the relationship, she sent him her "long, long adieu."[1]   The poem would have had to be written some two or three years after Carlyle and Margaret Gordon had ended whatever relationship they had had between their meeting in 1818 and this final parting in 1820, but since Carlyle had first met Jane Welsh in 1821, the poem may stand as a final emotional farewell to the previous relationship.[2] In fact, when Carlyle wrote about Margaret Gordon in his *Reminiscences*, he recalled, "To me, who had only known her for a few months, and who within a twelve or fifteen months saw the last of her, she continued for perhaps some three years a figure hanging more or less in my fancy, on the usual romantic, or latterly quite elegiac and silent terms . . ." (II, 57).

Other dates for "Adieu" are also possible, however. For example, although it cannot be regarded as absolutely accurate, Carlyle's own placement of the poem in "Fractions" — between "The Sower's Song" and "The Beetle" — argues for a date between 1826 and 1830. The phrase from Ecclesiastes 9:11 that time and chance happen to all men, on the other hand, points to early 1833 as a possibility since the phrase was on Carlyle's mind then as he uses it in three letters of January and February.[3] Finally, the manuscript paper on which the poem is written is watermarked 1836, a fact that J. A. S. Barrett's note on the poem takes to indicate that the manuscript is a copy of a much earlier one. All things considered, the safest dating for the poem seems to be Tennyson's "By December 1833" ("Poetry," p. 164).

"Adieu" is the only one of Carlyle's love poems that he published with his name.[4]

Composition: [By December, 1833?].

Manuscript: Yale University (watermark 1836).

First Publication: *Essays*, 2nd ed. (1840), III, 269-270.

Texts Consulted: MS; *Essays*, 2nd ed. (1840), III, 269-270; *Essays*, People's Edition (1872), VI, (Vol. I of *Critical and Miscellaneous Essays*), 291-292.

Copy-text: MS.

Textual Notes: The Yale manuscript is undated and untitled, but is watermarked 1836: it is the only extant manuscript of the poem. No substantive variants appear in any of the texts, and only one variant in accidentals appears between the second edition and the People's Edition.

Variant:

21   soul] soul, (People's Edition)

Citations:

[1]Quoted in Raymond Clare Archibald, *Carlyle's First Love* (London: John Lane, 1910), p. 76. For the story of Carlyle and Margaret Gordon's relationship, see Archibald, pp. 62-85.

[2]Wilson also makes this point in *Mr. Froude and Carlyle* (New York: Dodd, Mead, 1898), pp. 118-120.

[3]To Carlyle's brothers Alexander (27 January, 1833) and John (10 February, 1833), and to Leigh Hunt (28 February, 1833); printed in *Letters*, VI, 306, 320, and 337 respectively.

[4]The poem was also fairly widely anthologized in the past. It is also the only one of Carlyle's poems known to have been set to music and published as a popular song: Francesco Paolo Tosti published it as "Adieu, My Dear" (London: Chappell, 26 October, 1887).

31
To-Day

Commentary: Probably Carlyle's most popular poem, "To-Day" was frequently anthologized in the past and often used as a "Selection for Memorizing" in schools — no doubt because of its vintage Carlyle exhortation to work.[1]   As for "Adieu" the best dating for the poem is Carlyle's own of 1823-1833, and within that period D. A. Wilson believes (but gives no reason for his belief) that 1830 is the likely year (*Carlyle to "The French Revolution,"* p. 170). The theme is one that recurs throughout Carlyle's works, and is one that is fundamental to *Sartor Resartus* (1833-1834). In a letter of 24 March, 1833, Carlyle states his theme to his brother John in language that seems to argue for 1833 as a more probable year for the composition of "To-Day":

> . . . the only clear duty of Man lies in *this,* and nothing else: *Work*; work wisely while it is called today. Nothing in this universe now frightens me, tho' yearly it grows more stupendous, more divine; and the terrestrial *Life* appointed us more poor and brief. Eternity looks grander and kinder, if Time grow meaner and more hostile. I defy Time and the Spirit of Time: *I* (this *I*) am of Eternity, and shall return thither! (*Letters,* VI, 366)

Composition: [By December, 1833?].

Manuscript: National Library of Scotland MS 8992.173 (a copy of the poem in Jane Carlyle's handwriting, signed by Carlyle).

First Publication: Essays, 2nd ed. (1840), III, 271-272.

Texts Consulted: MS; *Essays,* 2nd ed.; *Essays,* People's Edition (1872), VI (Vol. I of *Critical and Miscellaneous Essays*), 291-292.

Copy-text: Essays, 2nd ed.

Textual Notes: The only manuscript of the poem is the undated manuscript at the National Library of Scotland. It is in Jane's handwriting, but is signed "T. Carlyle" in Carlyle's hand. The manuscript seems to be something that Jane produced for an autograph seeker, and it reflects her habits of capitalization rather than Carlyle's. The printings in the second edition and the People's Edition of the *Essays* are identical, with the single exception noted below.

Variants:

TO-DAY] TODAY (People's Edition)

2   Day] day (MS)

6   Day] day (MS)

6   is] was (MS)

14   Day] day (MS)

Citation:

[1] As G. B. Tennyson notes, the poem may have been a development from the verse motto to "Signs of the Times" (1829) which Carlyle translated from Goethe's paraphrase of Maucroix ("Poetry," p. 168n.). See also D. A. Wilson, *Carlyle to "The French Revolution,"* p. 104 and Leonard L. Mackall, "Verse von Frau Carlyle unter Goethes Gedichten an Personen," *Goethe Jahrbuch,* 25 (1904), 236.

32
Fortuna

Commentary: As is the case with the preceding two poems, the date of "Fortuna" is uncertain, and Carlyle's dating of 1823-1833 provides his only statement with respect to composition. Within Carlyle's framework David Masson assigns the poem to the Comley Bank years in Edinburgh (1826-1828),[1] but Carlyle's roughly chronological placement of the poem as the last of the "Fractions" suggests that 1833 might be a more likely date.

Composition: [By December, 1833?].

Manuscript: Untraced.

First Publication: *Essays,* 2nd ed. (1840), III, 272-273.

Texts Consulted: *Essays,* 2nd ed.; *Essays,* People's Edition, (1872), VI (Vol. I of *Critical and Miscellaneous Essays*), 283.

Copy-text: *Essays,* 2nd ed.

Textual Notes: The printings in the second edition and the People's Edition are identical.

Citation:

[1] Masson, p. 333.

33
To a Swallow Building Under Our Eaves

Commentary: Froude found the manuscript of this poem in Jane Carlyle's portfolio and printed it as a poem of hers that she had sent to Jeffrey as her complaint over her lot at Craigenputtoch (II, 235-236). Alexander Carlyle, however, writes that although the manuscript was in Jane's handwriting, it was endorsed "copied by Jane" in Carlyle's hand; he further states that Mary Carlyle (his wife), who had lived with Carlyle from 1868 until his death, had initialed the poem "T. C." in her copy of Froude's *Life,* and he dates the poem between 13 April, and 8 May, 1834 (*Love Letters,* II, 359-360n.).

The poem was dated 1834 in the manuscript, but its theme had been articulated before the Craigenputtoch period as early as 1824, when in a letter of 20 December Carlyle writes to Jane, "The very sparrow earns for itself a livelihood, beneath the eaves of the cottage: if *I* the illustrious Mr Thomas Carlyle cannot, then let me be sent to the Australian continent directly" (*Letters,* III, 232).[1]

Composition: [April-May, 1834?].

Manuscript: Untraced.

First Publication: Froude (1882), II, 291-292.

Texts Consulted: Froude; *Love Letters,* II, 358-359.

Copy-text: *Love Letters.*

Textual Notes: The manuscript that Alexander Carlyle and Froude both used as the basis for their printed texts is untraced at present. Alexander Carlyle wrote that the manuscript was in Jane's hand but endorsed "copied by Jane" by Carlyle and that the manuscript was dated "The Desert, 1834" (*Love Letters,* II, 360n.). Froude printed twenty-nine variants in substantives and accidentals; and since the manuscript is not available for study, his substantive variants are listed below.

Variants:

4	Bird] bird (Froude)
9	!] ,
12	!] .
17	!] .
26	*working*] working
26	*task*] task
29	Bird] bird
30	!] .
31	got,] got
32	wise,] wise .
34	Desert] desert
36	!] .

37   Bird!] bird;
38   !] .
39   !] ;
42   it] I

Citation:

[1] The same theme appears in similar language in letters of 25 March, 1825 (*Letters*, III, 309) and of 19 July, 1826 (*Letters*, IV, 116). Birds still nest under the eaves of Craigenputtoch, but Mr. George Armour the present owner says that they are house martins; the swallows now nest in the barn.

34
[Thirty-Nine English Articles]

Commentary: This poem was written in Carlyle's journal on 11 May, 1835 after John Sterling had given him F. D. Maurice's booklet on the Thirty-Nine Articles and the admission of dissenters to Oxford. The journal entry preceding the poem records that Carlyle had had a long talk with John Sterling about the pamphlet "by one Morris," and the entry continues, "What have I to do with that? An earnest man's earnest word was worth reading: my verdict lay in those four lines of jingle; which I, virtuously, spared Sterling the sight of . . ." (*Letters*, VIII, 139n.). The lines of "jingle" were "Thirty-nine English Articles," which immediately follow in the journal.[1]

Carlyle's objection to the Oxford movement was the same objection to formalized religion that he voiced in *Sartor Resartus*: that a concern with ritual denotes a hollow materialism rather than a vital spiritual faith. Moncure Conway gives one of many available examples of Carlyle's criticism of formal religion when he quotes a conversation in which Carlyle complained, "The Clergy are trying to make up for the vacancy left by the decay of all real Belief with theatrical displays, candles, and costumes. Everything goes to the theatre."[2] Conway also writes that Carlyle "acknowledged that the English Church was 'the apotheosis of decency,' but they who looked upon its articles as thirty-nine pillars of the universe were apt to find those pillars toppling upon them before this Samson. The sects, for him, remained to the end, each some small umbrella which its devotees imagined to be the vault of heaven."[3]   For a later poem in the same vein see "The Builder of this Universe" in this edition.

Composition: [11 May, 1835?]

Manuscript: Private hands.

First Publication: Froude (1884), I, 40.

Texts Consulted: Froude; *Froude's Life of Carlyle*, abridged and ed. John Clubbe (Columbus, Ohio: Ohio State University Press, 1979), pp. 338-339; *Letters*, VIII, 139-140n.

Copy-text: *Letters*.

Gloss:

  2   *particles*: In addition to the reference to the Articles of Religion, Carlyle may be playing on the ecclesiastical meaning of *particle* as 'the portion of the Host given to each lay communicant' (*OED*).

Textual Notes; John Clubbe prints his text from a copy of Froude's *Life* that had been owned and annotated by Alexander and Mary Carlyle, and Clubbe gives their date for the poem as 26 May, 1836, although Alexander Carlyle dates it in a marginal annotation as 11 May, 1835. Since the editors of *Letters* quote more of the surrounding journal material than does Froude, and since their text of the poem differs slightly from those previously published, it seems clear that the editors have recently gained access to the manuscript of this portion of Carlyle's journal; their text was therefore chosen as copy-text.   During the early days of their acquaintance Carlyle frequently misspells "Maurice" as "Morris."

Emendation:

  6   M[aurice]'s] (Clubbe); Maurice's (Froude); M— —s's (The *Letters'* printing reflects the pronunciation of Maurice's name as "Morris"; see *Letters*, VIII, 139n.).

Variants:

  3   his] His (Clubbe)

  3   Universe] universe (Froude, Clubbe)

  3   *you*] you (Froude)

Citations:

  [1] Froude indents the first and second, and fourth and fifth lines to show how six lines can be taken as four (*Life in London*, I, 40).

  [2] *Thomas Carlyle* (New York: Harper and Brothers, 1881), p. 79.

  [3] Ibid., p. 78.   In a letter of 25 December, 1837, to John Sterling,

Carlyle added a fortieth article. After writing that the devil's name is "Darkness" and that the blackest darkness is self-conceit, Carlyle writes, "Fear no seeing man, therefore; know that *he* is of Heaven, whoever else be not; that the Arch-Enemy, as I say, is the Arch-stupid; I call this my Fortieth Church Article,—which absorbs into it, and covers up in silence, all the other Thirty-nine!" (*Letters,* IX, 381).

35
Song I

Commentary: G. B. Tennyson argues for 1834 as the date for this and the following two "songs," largely on the basis of the increasing enmity that Carlyle held for Thomas Campbell and Francis Jeffrey, the subjects of Songs I and II, respectively ("Poetry," pp. 178-179n.). J. A. S. Barrett's notes on the poems, however, suggest 1838-1840 as the period of composition, and "Song III" seems to offer support for Barrett's dating.

Carlyle succeeded Thomas Campbell as a writer for Brewster's *Edinburgh Encyclopaedia* in 1820 and supported himself by writing articles for Brewster until 1823 (*Letters,* I, 229n.). Although he had been an admirer of Campbell earlier, when he actually met Campbell during his first trip to London, Carlyle formed an unfavorable opinion that did not essentially alter later in life. He gives a description of his first meeting with Campbell in a letter to Jane written 23 June, 1824:

> I have also seen Thomas Campbell: him I like worst of all. He is heartless as a little Edinburgh Advocate; there is a smirk on his face which would befit a shopman or an auctioneer; his very eye has the cold vivacity of a conceited worldling. His talk is small, contemptuous and shallow: the blue frock and trowsers, the eye glass, the wig, the very fashion of his bow proclaim the literary dandy.
>
> .   .   .   .
>
> The aspect of that man jarred the music of my mind for a whole day. He promised to invite me to his first "literary dejeuner": curiosity attracts, disgust repels; I know now whether will be stronger when the day arrives. Perhaps I

am hasty about Campbell; perhaps I am too severe; he was
my earliest favourite; I hoped to have found him different.
(*Letters,* III, 85)

Composition: [1838-1840?].

Manuscript: Yale University.

First Publication: Tennyson, "Poetry," pp. 178-179.

Texts Consulted: MS; Tennyson.

Copy-text: MS.

Gloss:

4   *pension*: Campbell was awarded a pension in 1805 for
        writing *The Pleasures of Hope* (Tennyson, "Poetry," p. 179).

Textual Notes: All three of the "Songs" are written on the same piece
of paper, and these Yale manuscripts provide the only authoritative
texts for the poems. The manuscripts are not among Carlyle's
clearer ones, and ambiguities in them account for the variants
from Tennyson that are listed here and following the next two
poems.

Variants:

2   bramble] wamble (Tennyson)
8   sulkily] milkily

36
Song II

Commentary: Carlyle met Francis Jeffrey in 1827 when Jeffrey was
editor of the *Edinburgh Review,* and the meeting was an important
one for Carlyle: Jeffrey gave Carlyle access to the pages of a major
periodical, and his essays that appeared in the *Edinburgh Review*
formed the early foundation of Carlyle's success. Jeffrey and
Carlyle's relationship was not always an idyllic one, however,
and before and after their break in 1834 over Jeffrey's refusal to
recommend Carlyle for available posts at the University of Edin-
burgh, Carlyle voiced the same sort of criticism of Jeffrey as appear
in "Song II."[1] Carlyle recalled his past thoughts about Jeffrey
in the reminiscence that he wrote in 1867:

I used to think to myself, "Here is a man whom they have
kneaded into the shape of an *Edinburgh Reviewer,* and
clothed the soul of in Whig formulas, and blue-and-yellow;
but he might have been a beautiful Goldoni, too, or some-

thing better in that kind, and have given us beautiful *Comedies,* and aerial pictures, true and lyric, of Human Life in a far other way!"[2]

Composition: [1838-1840?].

Manuscript: Yale University.

First Publication: Tennyson, "Poetry," p. 180.

Texts Consulted: MS; Tennyson

Copy-text: MS.

Textual Notes: See notes to "Song I."

Emendations:

   13   and] Tennyson; &
   14   Rather] Tennyson; rather

Variants:

   2   Thou] More (Tennyson)
   6   exclaim,] exclaim
   10   small much] This is written above the line over a cancelled "little" in the manuscript; a caret appears beneath the cancellation.
   13   Blue] blue
   13   Yellow] yellow

Citations:

[1]In 1831, for instance, when on 31 August Carlyle writes about Jeffrey in a letter to Jane:

> On the whole, were it not for the franks (which *are* an immense blessing) I might as well discontinue my attendance at Jermyn Street, where positively there is no good to be got, not so much as a serious word. The man is really, I suppose, very busy; farther I take his friendship for me, as I have all along done, to be perhaps three parts palabra, and one part half-sentiment, half-goodwill. Poor Duke! I will always love him: nevertheless there are two things I vehemently desire: first that I had £60 to pay him; secondly that I had my Wife's picture out of his hands, which I cannot but think are nowise worthy to hold it. (*Letters,* V, 382)

[2]*Reminiscences,* II, 272. Blue and yellow were the colors of the *Edinburgh Review* and of the Whig party for which it was an organ. Carlyle gave his opinion of Whigs in general in a letter to Mill of 28 October, 1833:

Unbelieving mediocrity, barren, dead and deathgiving, speaks itself forth more and more in all they do and dream. The true Atheist in these days is the Whig; he worships and can worship nothing but Respectability; and this he *knows,* unhappy man, to be—nothing but a two-wheeled vehicle! (*Letters,* VII, 22-23)

37
Song III

Commentary: "Song III" offers the strongest support for Barrett's 1838-1840 dating of the "Songs." The phrase "Lectured unto men" may be a general reference to the didactic qualities of *Sartor Resartus* (which was indeed a revolutionary book), as Tennyson argues ("Poetry," p. 181), but if one takes such phrases literally, then the weight of evidence is on Barrett's side. Carlyle gave his first series of lectures in May, 1837, for which he received £135 (*Letters,* IX, 214), and followed with other lecture series in 1838, 1839, and 1840. The "Revolution" that is mentioned in the poem can just as easily refer to *The French Revolution,* which was also published in May, 1837, and of which sales in England were slow.[1] Similarly, *Sartor Resartus,* after its generally poor reception when published serially in *Fraser's* (1833-1834) and publication in book form in the United States in 1836 (with some financial success), was not published in book form in England until 1838, and the venture was not profitable for Carlyle or the publisher: hence the comment "then came no money."[2]

Composition: [1838-1840?].

Manuscript: Yale University.

First Publication: Tennyson, "Poetry," p. 180.

Texts Consulted: MS; Tennyson, "Poetry"; Tennyson, *Sartor,* Frontispiece.

Copy-text: MS.

Gloss:

[1]*Cairel*: Barrett's notes say that this was an early Dumfries pronunciation of "Carlyle."

Textual Notes: The manuscript of "Song III" is the most difficult of the "Songs" to decipher, and this fact is reflected in Tennyson's change of mind in his two previous printings. See notes to "Song I."

Variants:

1   *Cairel*] Cairel (Tennyson, *Sartor*)
14] What looks to have been "tract" is cancelled following "published" in the manuscript.
14   they] thy (Tennyson, "Poetry"); my (Tennyson, *Sartor*)
14   thence] theme (Tennyson, "Poetry"; *Sartor*)
16   Sense] teme (Tennyson, "Poetry"; *Sartor*)

Citations:

[1] See for instance *Letters*, IX, 343.
[2] Thomas Carlyle, *Letters to His Youngest Sister*, ed. Charles Townsend Copeland (1899; rpt. Hildesheim: Georg Olms, 1968), p. 113. Also see *Letters*, IX, 365.

38
[Cock-a-Doodle-Doo]

Commentary: This little poem was written in a letter to John Sterling on 27 September, 1841 as a response to a lithograph left by Sterling and satirizing Carlyle and some of his teachings.[1] In the letter Carlyle writes, "Infinitely obliged by your Lithograph; which pours a flood of light for me over the error of my ways! By Heaven's mercy we shall not be lost for want of warning. *Humanum est errare; Sterlingianum edocere.*"[2]

Composition: 27 September, 1841.

Manuscript: National Library of Scotland MS. 531.40 (the letter to John Sterling; printed in *Letters of Thomas Carlyle to John Stuart Mill, John Sterling and Robert Browning*, ed. Alexander Carlyle [London: T. Fisher Unwin, 1923], p. 248.

First Publication: *Letters of Thomas Carlyle to John Stuart Mill, John Sterling, and Robert Browning*, ed. Alexander Carlyle (London: T. Fisher Unwin, 1923), p. 248.

Texts Consulted: MS; *Letters of Thomas Carlyle to John Stuart Mill, John Sterling, and Robert Browning*.

Copy-text: MS.

Textual Notes: The National Library of Scotland manuscript provides the only authoritative text for this poem.

Citations:

[1] *Letters of Thomas Carlyle to John Stuart Mill, John Sterling, and Robert Browning*, ed. Alexander Carlyle (London: T. Fisher Unwin, 1923), p. 247n.

In a letter of 31 October, 1841, Carlyle wrote to Sterling about the fate of the lithograph:

> The Lithograph cockadoodle is not here now, did not stay here above a day; packing up a mass of abominable scarecrow effigies of Oxford Puseyites for Thomas Spedding, I found the Lithograph still lying on my table, and put it in by way of salt, to give a kind of savour to the mass, and perhaps keep off putrescence. So Spedding has it,—and who knows accordingly but future ages will have it! A man must look to that when he lithographs. Prince Posterity is always on the watch withal, if anything be going! (Ibid., pp. 248-249)

[2] Ibid., pp. 247-248. *Humanum est errare; Sterlingianum edocere* might be translated as "To err is human; to instruct is Sterling."

39
[The Lasses of the Canongate]

Commentary: The poem is from the manuscript notes concerning Oliver Cromwell and the Battle of Dunbar. This section of the manuscript is dated and commented upon by Carlyle: "7 October 1841.—Dull still, as ditchwater and dark as chaos." The poem is illustrative of how close Carlyle was to the ballad tradition and its narrative similarities in prose. See Fielding, pp, 6-13.

Composition: 7 October, 1841.

Manuscripts: Forster Collection, Victoria and Albert Museum.

First Publication: Unpublished.

Texts Consulted: MS.

Copy-text: MS.

Gloss:

1   *Canongate*: A section of old Edinburgh where Cromwell stayed upon entering the City on September 7, 1650, and where he took up headquarters during the rest of his campaign in Scotland.

2   *Leslie*: General David Lesley, defeated at Dunbar on 3
      September, 1650.

5   *Colrunspath*: No doubt Carlyle means Cockburnspath,
      the only road leading from Dunbar to England, where
      Cromwell engaged the Scots forces on September 3, 1650.
      In his note to Letter CXXXV in *Oliver Cromwell,* Carlyle
      says, "'Copperspath' . . . is the country pronunciation of
      Cockburnspath; the name of a wild rock-and-river chasm,
      through which the great road goes, some miles to the east-
      ward of Dunbar" (*Works,* II, 180).

7   *skailed*: 'to scatter, especially to rout.'

8   *wae*: 'sorrowful.'

8   *tine*: 'lose.'

Textual Notes: The manuscript provides the only text for this poem.
The transcription was provided by K. J. Fielding.

Emendation:

11   friends'] friends

21   lovers'] lovers

21   horses'] horses

40
[Gae 'Wa Wi]

Commentary: See notes for "Lasses of the Canongate," entry no. 39.
This particular poem appears in some of the notes that Carlyle
made for *Oliver Cromwell.* It comes in the second act of Carlyle's
outline of "*Oliver Cromwell* as a Drama," in the scene when the
legendary Jenny Geddes hurls her stool at the minister in St.
Giles High Kirk.

Composition: [Near October, 1842].

Manuscript: Forster Collection, Victoria and Albert Museum, MS 103r.

First Publication: K. J. Fielding, ed. "Unpublished Manuscripts—II:
Carlyle's Scenario for *Cromwell,*" *Carlyle Newsletter,* no. 2 (March,
1980), p. 9.

Texts Consulted: MS; Fielding.

Copy-text: MS.

Gloss:

1   *kistfu whistles*:   kist can mean a 'chest, basket, or even cof-

fin,' but the expression as a whole is likely from Scots dialect. A "kist o' whistles" is a 'church organ.'

3　　　*soubristles*: 'sow's bristles, literally the stiff hairs on a hog's back, often likened to the hair on a man's face.'

4　　　*ava*: 'at all.'

Textual Notes: The transcript of the manuscript and the date were provided by K. J. Fielding, who has set the stanzaic form given here. In the manuscript the poem is written out with the use of slashes and is enclosed in parentheses.

Variants:

3]　　written above the line: "dead as swine-thistles"

4]　　written above the line: "The sheep winna eat"

41
[The Builder of This Universe]

Commentary: Carlyle added "The Builder of this Universe" to the manuscript that served as the printer's copy of *Past and Present* (1843).[1] Like "Thirty-nine English Articles" the poem presents a criticism of the Oxford Movement, which Carlyle saw as representative of the contrast between the vitality of twelfth-century Catholicism and the hollowness of contemporary religious practice. Following the poem Carlyle wrote,

> That certain human souls, living on this practical Earth, should think to save themselves and a ruined world by noisy theoretic demonstrations and laudations of *the* Church, instead of some unnoisy, unconscious, but *practical,* total, heart-and-soul demonstration of *a* Church: this, in the circle of revolving ages, this also was a thing we were to see.[2]

Composition: 1842.

Manuscript: Yale University.

First Publication: *Past and Present* (1843), p. 159.

Texts Consulted: MS; *Past and Present* (1843; 2nd ed., 1845; People's Ed., 1872).

Copy-text: *Past and Present* (2nd ed., 1845), p. 159.

Textual Notes: The Yale manuscript provides the earliest version of the poem, which was then revised in proof before the first edition of

Past and Present was published. The second edition is used as copy-text here because it seems to represent Carlyle's final intention.

Variants:

2   planets,] worlds and (MS)

3   all] His (1843)

3   by,] by (1843)

3   The great Groundplan He shap'd Creation by (MS); "great" is written above the cancelled "one" in the MS.

Citations:

[1] The manuscript of the first draft of *Past and Present* is in the British Library, and that of the printer's copy is at Yale. The poem does not appear in the British Library manuscript, but was added to the printer's copy on a separate small piece of paper which was pasted to the left margin of page 48 of the manuscript. For a complete discussion of Carlyle's method of composition for *Past and Present,* see Grace J. Calder, *The Writing of Past and Present* (New Haven: Yale University Press, 1949), where part of her discussion of the added material is the following:

> The presence of odd-sized pieces of paper pasted on full folios, a phenomenon peculiar to the Printer's Copy, deserves explanation. Some of the small pieces provide space for re-wording passages when the sheet itself already bears one or two deleted versions. Most of the addenda, however, instead of replacing earlier forms of passages, add new material. The physical format of the manuscript thus gives palpable proof that Carlyle habitually expanded his thought —if not his thought, then its expression. (p. 118)

Calder also notes that the portion of the manuscript that contains the poem is dated "7 Decr 1842" (p. 19).

[2] *Past and Present* (London: Chapman and Hall, 1843), p. 159.

42
[Unused to Trade]

Commentary: This little poem was apparently written to accompany a Christmas present that Carlyle gave to Jane in 1847. Following the poem Carlyle wrote, "All good attend my Darling, thro' this

dim gulf of Time, and thro' the big Ocean it is leading to. Amen,
Amen." It is possible that the poem reflects the continual dis-
agreements the Carlyles had over finances, principally because
of Carlyle's niggardly moods. See for example Jane's "Missive
on the Budget," also entitled "BUDGET of a Femme incomprise,"
owned by the Bodleian Library and written on 12 February,
1855. The opening paragraph of the letter reads:

> I dont choose to *speak* again on the *Money-question.*
> The "replies" from the Noble Lord are unfair, and unkind,
> and little to the purpose. When you tell me I "pester your
> life out about *money*"—that "your soul is sick with hearing
> about it"—that I "had better make the money I *have* serve,
> at all rates—hang it!—let *you* alone of it;" *all that* I call
> perfectly unfair, the reverse of kind, and tending to nothing
> —but disagreement—

Jane goes on to postulate an elaborate and witty defense for her
spending. Carlyle appends the following note to the letter: "The
enclosed was read with great laughter (had been found lying on
my table, as I returned out of the porty garden from smoking);
— 'debt' is already paid off . . . and all is settled to poor Goody's
heart's content."

Composition: 25 December, 1847.

Manuscript: Carlyle'House, London, MS, 275.

First Publication: Unpublished.

Texts Consulted: MS.

Copy-text: MS.

Textual Notes: The London manuscript provides the only text for this
poem. The manuscript is addressed "Jane W. Carlyle" on the out-
side, and the poem is dated "25 decr, 1847—" and signed "T.
Carlyle[.]"

Notes to
Autograph Poems and Questionable Attributions
for Thomas Carlyle

1
[Little Did My Mother Think]

Commentary: There are several versions of this old Scots poem. In the
version in the *Two Note Books* (p. 55), Carlyle writes in dialect
what was subsequently to become known as his "Windowpane
Verse." The poem was scratched on a windowpane at 3 Moray
Street, Edinburgh, Carlyle's lodging while a student at Edinburgh
University. The pane was sold at auction at Sotheby's in July
of 1896 for £11.5s. The probable sources are two ballads, "The
Queen's Marie" and "Mary Hamilton." In the former, Marie, a
French waiting-woman to Mary Queen of Scots, becomes pregnant
by Henry Darnley and after delivering is brought to trial in Edin-
burgh by the Queen. The final stanza, spoken by Marie, is as
follows:

> "O little did my mother ken,
> The day she cradled me,
> The lands I was to travel in
> Or the death I was to die."

In the latter poem "Mary Hamilton," from the west of Scotland,
Mary drowns her illicit baby and is hanged for the crime. Her
lines are as follows:

> "O little did my mother think
> The day she prinned my gown
> That I was to come sae frae hame
> To be hanged in Edinburgh Town."

In the *Two Note Books* Carlyle suggests a third source: "Extract
by Burns—*first* come to me thro' T. Murray" (p. 55n.).

Composition: 31 December, 1823.

Manuscript: Carlyle House, London (etched on a windowpane).

First Publication: *Athenaeum*, No. 3179 (29 September, 1888), 420.

Texts Consulted: *Athenaeum*; *The Critic* (NY), 28 (June, 1896), 470;
Notes & Queries, Sers. 8, Vol. 9 (September 19, 1896), 237, and
(October 10, 1896), 301.

Copy-text: MS.

Textual Notes: None of the above texts consulted can be considered
authorized, and each varies somewhat from the printed text. They
are listed here for point of reference only.

2
[O Busk Ye]

Commentary: This poem cannot be considered original to Carlyle, although often attributed to him. Miller says that it is a version of an older ballad "Jonny Cock" (p. 163); and Carlyle attributes it to one entitled "Johnnie o' Braidislea." Carlyle says that he hummed this ballad, often sung to him by his mother, as he approached London in 1834 (*Reminiscences,* I, 99).

Composition: [1834?]. Written out by Carlyle on 3 June, 1866.

Manuscript: National Library of Scotland, MS 532.

First Publication: *Reminiscences.*   Ed. James A. Froude (London: Longmans, 1881), II, 171.

Texts Consulted: MS; *Reminiscences*; *Reminiscences* (Norton), I, 99; Miller, p. 63.

Copy-text: MS.

Textual Notes: Miller adds two lines to the beginning of the poem ("O Busk ye, O busk ye, my three bluidy hounds, / O buske ye, and go with me,"); and he drops Carlyle's remark ("and shoot down") in the last line.

3
[What is Heaven?]

Commentary: The poem is in the hand of James Ellis and is signed "S——"; and is written on the front endpaper of a first English edition of *Sartor Resartus.* It is then signed "T. Carlyle[.]" It is possible, although not certain, that this James Ellis is related to the Carlyle family (see *Letters,* I, 139). The poem does display some of the promethean spark of Carlyle, yet direct attribution cannot be established. The date, 1838, is chosen for composition since it is the publication date of the edition of *Sartor* in question. The date, however, must be considered tentative.

Composition: [1838?].

Manuscript: Private hands.

First Publication: Unpublished.

Texts Consulted: MS.

Copy-text: MS.

Textual Notes: The manuscript provides the only text for this poem.
Emendations:

3	and] &
14	and] &
16	and] &

Variant:

10]   "(waken)" is written above "leaves" in the manuscript.

4

Dirge: "Fear No More'

Commentary: On 22 September, 1872 William Allingham writes in his
    diary that he had visited Carlyle at three o'clock and that Car-
    lyle had quoted the following lines from Shakespeare's *Cymbeline*:

> Fear no more the heat o' th' sun
> Nor the furious winter's rages'
> Thou thy worldly task hast done,
> Home art gone and ta'en thy wages.
>   (IV, ii, 258-261)

Allingham also writes that Carlyle had commented that the passage
was "One of the prettiest things ever written" and the "It is like
the distant tinkle of evening bells. Much comes of the rhymes—
rhymes are valuable sometimes, answering somehow to the melody
within a man's thought and soul."[1]
    The passage from Shakespeare was an enduring favorite of
Carlyle's, which he frequently chose to write out for autograph
seekers and which Froude wrote that Carlyle often recited towards
the end of his life (*Life in London*, II, 279). Moreover, twenty-
four years before Allingham's diary entry Carlyle had used Shake-
speare's lines to frame two stanzas of his own "Dirge."

Composition: November, 1848.

Manuscript: Yale University.

First Publication: Unpublished.

Texts Consulted: MS.

Copy-text: MS.

Textual Notes: The Yale manuscript provides the only text of the
    poem. Barrett's notes say that the poem was "copied in fac-
    simile for private circulation," but the editors have been unable

to confirm this. The poem is titled "Dirge: 'Fear no More'" on the verso of the manuscript, and the manuscript is dated "November 1848" in the left margin opposite the poem.

Citation:

[1] *A Diary,* ed. H[elen] Allingham and D. Radford (1907; rpt. London: Macmillan, 1908), p. 210.

5
[Simon Brodie]

Commentary: Another favorite of autograph seekers, this poem exists in many versions. The one here is from the Houghton Library and is signed and dated "Chelsea 23 janry 1849." Other manuscripts of the poem are at Yale University, and are dated "20 decr, 1852" and "19 decr, 1859" respectively. For a discussion of the history of the ballad and its variants, see J. W. E., "Carlyle as a Poet," *Notes and Queries,* Series 5, Vol. 6 (August 5, 1876), 110. See also Nicholl, p. 173.

Composition: 23 January, 1849.

Manuscript: Harvard University.

First Publication: *Autographic Mirror* (1862), II, 162.

Texts Consulted: Harvard University MS; Yale University MSS; *Autographic Mirror.*

Copy-text: Harvard MS.

Textual Notes: Since the poem is not original with Carlyle, no versions carry authorial sanction. The example printed in this edition was selected as the earliest.

6
[Einsam, Einsam]

Commentary: This poem may also be by Carlyle. He wrote it in a letter of 3 April, 1849, to Jane, who was visiting with the Ashburtons; but because of Carlyle's wide familiarity with German literature, the fact that the poem is in German makes definite attribution of it to him hazardous, even though he did write at least one poem in German. Certainly the sentiment that the poem

expresses is fittingly Carlylean,[1] but in the absence of more sub-
stantial evidence the poem must be regarded as belonging to the
class of "possible."

Composition: 3 April, 1849.

Manuscript: National Library of Scotland MS 613.290 (an unpublished
letter to Jane, 3 April, 1849).

First Publication: Unpublished.

Texts Consulted: MS.

Copy-text: MS.

Gloss:

'Alone, alone, that I am not,
For the spirits of my loved ones,
Distant and dead,
They surround me.'

Textual Notes: The National Library of Scotland manuscript provides
the only text for this poem.

Citation:

[1]Carlyle used similar language in writing to his mother about his
deceased father and sister in a letter of 3 December, 1833, for
example:

Tomorrow I believe is my eight-and-thirtieth birthday!
You were then young in life; I had not yet entered it. Since
then—how much! how much! They are in the Land of
Silence (but while we live, not of Forgetfulness), whom we
once knew, and (often with thoughts too deep for words)
wistfully ask of their and our Father Above that we may
again know. God is great; God is good! It is written, "He
will wipe away all tears from every eye." Be it as He wills;
not as we wish.— These things continually almost dwell with
me; loved Figures hovering in the background or foreground
of my mind. A few years more, and we too shall be with
them in Eternity. Meanwhile it is this *Time* that is ours;
let us be busy with *it*; and work, work, "for the Night
cometh." (*Letters,* VII, 50)

7

Ilias (Americana) in Nuce

Commentary: "Ilias" is included here as a prose-poem since it is in
obvious parody of the ballad tradition. It reflects Carlyle's at-
titudes on the American Civil War. Bret Harte was so insulted by
Carlyle's "poem" that he penned one in response, published in the
San Francisco *Evening Bulletin* (8 September, 1863), p. 3, col. 5:

> "Peter of the North" to Thomas Carlyle.
> It's true that I hire my servant per day,
>> Per month, or per year—as he chooses;
> While "Paul of the South" takes his bondman for life,
>> Without asking if he refuses,
>
>>>>>>>>>> T. C.,
>
>> Without asking if he refuses!
>
>
> But if you judge of the merits alone,
>> We surely have the right to inquire
> The date of your service with "Paul of the South,"
>> And what is the length of your hire,
>
>>>>>>>>>> T. C.,
>
>> And what is the length of your hire!

Composition: May, 1863.

Manuscript: Untraced.

First Publication: *Macmillan's Magazine*, 8 (1863), 301.

Texts Consulted: *Macmillan's Magazine*.

Copy-text: *Macmillan's Magazine*.

Gloss:

> *Illias (Americana) in Nuce*: 'American Iliad in a nutshell.'

Textual Notes: *Macmillan's Magazine* provides the text for this poem.

8

[Wandering in a Strange Land]

Commentary: The poem is written in the rear flyleaf of a copy of the
Inaugural Address (1866), with the comment: "Paraphrased from
T. Carlyle by W. J. Fox." The poem is from a hymn book, and

Carlyle's involvement with it must be considered highly con-
jectural. The date is equally conjectural and is based upon the
publication date of the *Inaugural Address.*   The poem itself
is in a third hand.

Composition: [1866?].

Manuscript: Private hands.

First Publication: Unpublished.

Texts Consulted: MS.

Copy-text: MS.

Textual Notes: The manuscript provides the only text for this poem.

9
[There Was a Piper Had a Coo]

Commentary: Like "Simon Brodie," this poem is part of the large and
varied ballad tradition; for a discussion see under notes for "Simon
Brodie." An old Scottish nursery rhyme, this poem is purported
to have been sung to Carlyle as an infant by his mother.

Composition: 3 February, 1870.

Manuscript: Private hands.

First Publication: Notes and Queries, Series 5, Vol. 6 (July 22, 1876),
68.

Texts Consulted: Notes and Queries; Nicholl, p. 173; Froude (1884),
II, 362.

Copy-text: Notes and Queries.

Textual Notes: The *Notes and Queries* printing was selected as copy-
text because it is the oldest extant version of the poem, which
Carlyle apparently wrote out on more than one occasion. The
manuscript here was last owned by Jane Haig (see *Notes and
Queries,* Series 5, Vol. 6 [August 5, 1876], 110-111), and was
originally written out for the Rev. Thomas Alexander of Chelsea
on 3 February, 1870. The Nicholl and Froude texts differ slightly,
but are not deemed of substantive value because their authority
cannot be established.

Notes to the Translations of Thomas Carlyle

1
The Fisher

Commentary: This translation of Goethe's *Der Fischer* and the commentary attendant to it were forwarded to Jane, probably in a letter of 27 May, 1822. For further discussion, see notes under Jane's translation, entry no. 1.

Composition: [May, 1822].

Manuscript: National Library of Scotland, MS 529.21.

First Publication: *Letters* (1970), II, 121-122.

Texts Consulted: MS; *Letters*.

Copy-text: MS.

Textual Notes: Except for stanzas 3 and 7, which are Jane's and accepted by Carlyle as accurate, the translations are original. In the manuscript, only the sub-title is given, and it is underlined twice, except "by" which is underlined once. The manuscript is torn at the right-hand margin, obscuring some words in stanzas 6 and 8.

Emendations:

11	and] &
16	and] &
24	dew?"] dew?

2
Faust's Curse

Commentary: Carlyle records that when he saw his translation displayed in the window of the *Athenaeum* offices, he "hurried on with downcast eyes, as if I had seen myself in the Pillory" (*Two Note Books*, p. 232). Earlier, in a letter to Jane of 18 October, 1822, Carlyle calls his translation "truly Della-cruscan lines" (*Letters,* II, 177). Appended to the poem is the following comment by Carlyle: "('Our armies swore terribly in Flanders, but—it was nothing to this,' says the Corporal.)—T.C."

Composition: [October, 1822].

Manuscript: Untraced.

First Publication: *Chaos,* no. 30 [1830], 120.

Texts Consulted: *Chaos*; *Athenaeum,* no. 219 (7 January, 1832), 5; *Love Letters,* II, 351.

Copy-text: *Chaos.*

Textual Notes: The *Chaos* printing of the poem is dated "Edinb. 1813." and is signed "I.C." This would seem to indicate that the poem was printed from a copy in Jane's hand with an inferred but seemingly incorrect date. Tennyson points out that this is only one of two translations of the poem — the earlier version which appeared in "Faustus" (*New Edinburgh Review,* 2 [April, 1822], 316-334) is "lame in comparison" ("Poetry," p. 170). Tennyson also suggests a later date of October, 1822 for the translation "Faust's Curse," if one distinguishes between the two translations. The *Athenaeum* and Jones' printings, the latter follows the former for the most part, cancel lines 9-12, 17-20, and each places the appended note, which does not appear in the *Chaos* version, after the title. In the *Love Letters,* Alexander Carlyle prints in part the *Chaos* version, but alters the stanzaic presentation.

Variants:

1	If] "If, (*Love Letters*)
1	stealing] stealing, (*Athenaeum*)
2	stay'd] stay'd— (*Athenaeum*); stay'd, (*Love Letters*)
3	trace] touch (*Athenaeum*)
3	feeling] feeling, (*Athenaeum*)
4	betray'd;] betray'd,— (*Athenaeum*)
7	hearts] heart's (*Athenaeum, Love Letters*)
7	syrens] syrens, (*Athenaeum*)
13	all] all, (*Athenaeum*)
14	hopes our name from Death] hope from death our Name (*Athenaeum*)
15	*as ours* on Earth] as earthly Good (*Athenaeum*)
15	flatters] flatters, (*Athenaeum*)
16	child or wife] Wife or Child (*Athenaeum*)
16	plough or slave!] Plough or Slave; (*Athenaeum*)
17	mammon] Mammon (*Love Letters*)
18	deeds,] deeds; (*Love Letters*)
21	grapes] Grapes (*Athenaeum*)
22	thrill,] thrill (*Atheaneum*)
22	first!] first; (*Athenaeum*)
23	hoping] Hoping (*Athenaeum*)
23	believing!] Believing, (*Athenaeum*)

24   patience] Patience (*Athenaeum*)
24   curs'd!] curs'd!"– (*Athenaeum*)
Emendation:
7   hearts'] hearts

3
[Who Never Ate His Bread in Sorrow]

Commentary: Written out in a letter to Jane of 18 September, 1823, this translation Carlyle insists is "mediocre–the worst kind" (*Letters*, II, 434).

Composition: September, 1823.

Manuscript: National Library of Scotland MS 529.74 (the letter to Jane; printed in *Letters*, II, 434-435).

First Publication: *Wilhelm Meister* (1824), p. 214.

Texts Consulted: MS; *Wilhelm Meister* (1824); *Wilhelm Meister* (Rev. Ed., 1839); *Wilhelm Meister* (New Ed., 1842); *Wilhelm Meister* (People's Ed., 1874); *Letters*.

Copy-text: *Wilhelm Meister* (1842).

Textual Notes: In addition to the variants listed below, none of the lines in the *Letters* version is indented.

Variants:
2   hours] hours, (1824)
3   Weeping] Weeping, (*Letters*)
4   ye] you
5   earth] Earth
5   earth,] Earth,

4
Confessio Fidei

Commentary: Although happy about the progress of his *Life of Schiller*, Carlyle remained unconvinced about his skills as a writer; and, in a Journal entry for 7 January [1824], which precedes the poem, he writes, "*Shall* I learn to 'write with ease'–*ever* learn?" Whatever his intellectual traumas, this poem like those around it documents Carlyle's continuing interest in translation.

Composition: January [1824].

Manuscript: Private hands.

First Publication: *Two Note Books* (1898), pp. 61-63.

Texts Consulted: *Two Note Books*.

Copy-text: *Two Note Books*.

Gloss:

 Confessio Fidei: 'Confession of Faith.'

Textual Notes: Since the manuscript of Carlyle's Journal is presently unavailable to scholars, Norton's edited text in the *Two Note Books* must serve as the copy-text. And, although Norton does not take liberties with texts comparable to Froude and Alexander Carlyle, he did on occasion edit and/or emendate his materials. Carlyle gives this translation the complete title: "Confessio Fidei *of Wallensteins Jäger* (23)[.]"

Variants (above the uncancelled original):

1	mean]	proposed
3	To]	In
3	moment]	joys of the
3	trusting]	sharing
4]	[On the past or the future]	not thinking or caring
7	to]	mid
7	whistling]	thickest
8	red and roaring Rhine]	Rhine's wild roaring tide
10	without loss of time]	not minding a jot
11	and pray]	d'ye see
12	may have my way]	you'd let me be
15	happens the besom]	the rough rude
16	and sweeps one]	Pleases to shove us
22	springs]	falls
26	To]	From
26	he bids adieu]	must onward roam
28	vintage [time]]	laughing times of
30	then what goods or worth he]	In the place of goods of worth or self
31	If the soldier]	What has he unless
32	nothing of]	naught to call
32	creature]	fellow

5
[Where Lemon-Trees Do Bloom]

Commentary: The poem here is recited by Mignon, and appears as the lead for Book III, Chapter I, of *Wilhelm Meisters Lehrjahre*. Meister has become the surrogate father to Mignon, an orphan girl, whose poetic soul Carlyle describes in the 1824 Preface to the first edition as "of the earth, but not earthly" (p. xv). Mignon later dies of a broken heart after she is separated from Meister.

Composition: [1824].

Manuscripts: Yale University.

First Publication: *Wilhelm Meister* (1824), I, 229.

Texts Consulted: MSS; *Wilhelm Meister* (1824); *Wilhelm Meister* (Rev. Ed., 1839); *Wilhelm Meister* (New Ed., 1842); *Wilhelm Meister* (People's Ed., 1874).

Copy-text: *Wilhelm Meister* (People's Ed., 1874).

Textual Notes: The poem exists in six different versions: four published texts and two manuscripts. The manuscript versions seem to pre-date the first edition of 1824, although even this cannot be firmly established. The so-called "Revised Edition" of 1839 and the "New Edition, Revised" of 1842 contain substantive and accidental changes, one from the other, and each from the 1824 edition. The People's Edition of 1874 embodies further revision. Each translation has its merits; but, of course, it is impossible to arrive at a decision as to exactly what text Carlyle intended. Since the 1842 version and the People's Edition are relatively similar, and since they are the last two revised texts, the People's Edition has been selected as the copy-text. In this case the People's Edition represents authorical sanction. What these various texts illustrate, however, is that Carlyle himself was not sure of the best translation. In his 1839 Preface, for example, he observes that he "made many little changes," but laments that it like the 1824 first edition is "stiff and laboured" (pp. v-vi). The two manuscript versions are identified as MS1 and MS2, and the other texts by their dates of publication. To avoid confusion because of the numerous changes, the lines here are printed more fully than usual. At the top of MS1 is written: "(which is worse?)"; and at the top of MS2 is written: "(Another of the same.)[.]"

Variants:

1] Dost' know the land where fresh the citrons bloom, (MS1);"
Knowst thou the land where the fresh citrons bloom, (MS2);
Know'st thou the land where the lemon-trees bloom? (1824);
(1839 and 1842 as 1824, except "citron-apples bloom,")

2] Where glows the orange 'mid the thicket's gloom, (MS1);
And the gold-orange glows in the deep thicket's gloom;
MS2); Where the gold orange glows in the deep thicket's
gloom? (1824); gloom, (1839)

3] When winds are soft that from the blue hea'vn blow; (MS1);
Where a wind ever soft from the blue heaven blows, (MS3,
1824)

4] Where myrtles close and laurels stately grow? (MS1); And
the groves are of myrtle and laurel and rose? (MS2, 1824)

5] Dost know it well? (MS1); Knowst thou it? (MS2); Know'st
thou it? (1824); Know'st thou it then? (1839, 1842)

6] To it! to it (MS1); Thither! O Thither (MS2); Thither!
O thither, (1824); 'Tis there! 'Tis there, (1839, 1842)

7] With thee would I my loved one go. (MS1); My dearest
and kindest with thee would I go. (MS2); My dearest and
kindest, with thee I would go. (1824); O my true lov'd one,
thou with me must go! (1839, 1842)

8] Dost' know the house, its roof on pillars tall, (MS1); Knowst
thou the house with its porch-columns tall, (MS2); Know'st
thou the house, with its turretted walls, (1824)

9] The chambers bright, its lofty glancing hall, (MS1); With
its glittering chambers, and stately hall, (MS2); Where the
chambers are glancing, and vast are the halls? (1824)

10] Where marble statues look at me so mild (MS1); Where the
figures of marble look on me so mild (MS2); 1824 as MS2,
except comma after "mild"); (1839 and 1842 as copy-
text, except "each one" instead of "me on")

11] As if they said; "What harmed thee thus poor child?" (MS1);
As if thinking: "Why thus did they use thee poor child?"
(MS2); (1824 as MS2, except comma after "thee")

12] Dost' know it well? (MS1); Knowst thou it? (MS2); Know'st
thou it? (1824); Know'st thou it then? (1838, 1842)

13] To it! To it (MS1); Thither! O Thither (MS2); Thither! O
thither! (1824); 'Tis there! 'Tis there, (1839, 1842)

14] With thee would I my guardian go. (MS1); My guide and my guardian with thee would I go. (MS2); 1824 as MS2, except "thee, I would go"); O my protector, thou with me must go! (1839, 1842)

15] Dost' know the hill, its cliffs and cloudy ridge? (MS1); Knowst thou the mountain, its cloud-covered arch, (MS2); (1824 as MS2, except "Know'st" for Knowst")

16] The mule in mist steps o'er ["steps o'er" cancelled] treads slow that roaring bridge; (MS1); Where the mules among the mist o'er the wild torrent march [MS edge burned here] (MS2); (1824 as MS2, except "torrent-march?")

17] Old [cancelled] The Dragons ["s" cancelled] makes their [cancelled] her dens ["s" cancelled] within these caves; (MS1); In the clefts of it Dragons lie coil'd with their brood; (MS2); (1824 as MS2, except "it, dragons")

18] Rent crags rush down, and o'er them rush the waves. (MS1); The rent crag rushes down, and above it the flood. (MS2, 1824)

19] Dost' know it well? (MS1); Knowst thou it? (MS2); Know'st thou it? (1824); Know'st thou it then? (1839, 1842)

20] By it! By it! (MS1); Thither! O Thither (MS2); Thither! O thither! (1824); 'Tis there! Tis there, (1839, 1842)

21] Our way is: O! My father let us go. (MS1); Our way leadeth: Father. O come let us go. (MS2); (1824 aa MS2, except "Father!" and "go!")

6

The Village

Commentary: This poem is a translation of Gottfried August Bürger's "Das Dörfchen." G. B. Tennyson points out that "Carlyle has bowdlerized the German original," a poem in "praise of genteel rusticity climaxed by a description of a romp in a brook by both shepherd and shepherdess." Carlyle omits twenty-seven lines of the original and adds twenty-one lines of his own, by dropping Bürger's emphasis on sensual joy and adopting his on heavenly fulfillment. "Carlyle's liberty with the original," says Tennyson, "is greatest when the passage was likely to offend strict morality" ("Poetry," pp. 170-171).

Composition: [By October, 1825.].

Manuscript: Untraced.

First Publication: *Dumfries Monthly Magazine,* 1 (October, 1825), 332-333.

Texts Consulted: *Dumfries Monthly Magazine.*

Copy-text: *Dumfries Monthly Magazine.*

Textual Notes: The poem is headed "Translation from Bürger, T. C., 1825."

7
[Enweri Tells Us]

Commentary: In a letter to Jane of July, 1826, Carlyle quotes these lines after projecting "fifty kisses" from Jane and "catching [her] round the waist and stealing two kisses by way of Promethean fire from fairest lips in the world . . . (*Letters,* IV, 117). After quoting the poem, he adds, "Tolerance is the hardest for those that have it not by Nature; to 'bear one another's burdens,' to be true, patient, meek, humble, one in heart as we are to be in fate and interest (*Letters,* IV, 118).

Composition: July, 1826.

Manuscript: National Library of Scotland MS 532.90. (Letter to Jane, July, 1826; printed in *Letters,* IV, 118).

First Publication: *Wilhelm Meister's Travels* in *German Romance* (1827), IV, 35.

Texts Consulted: MS; *Wilhelm Meister's Travels* (1827); *Wilhelm Meister's Travels* (Rev. Ed., 1839); *Wilhelm Meister's Travels* (New Ed., 1842); *Wilhelm Meister's Travels* (People's Ed., 1874).

Copy-text: *Wilhelm Meister's Travels* (1842).

Textual Notes: The translation of the *Travels* was first published as volume four of the *German Romance,* a collection of short stories translated by Carlyle. It was then included with the *Apprenticeship* in subsequent editions of *Wilhelm Meister.*

Variants:

1   us, a] us (a (1842)
2   scan:] scan); (1842)
3   "In] At (1824); 'In (1874)
4   Tolerance."] Tolerance. (1842); Tolerance' (1874)

8
[For the Tie is Snapt Asunder]

Commentary: The poem appears in Chapter XIV of *Wilhelm Meister's Travels,* and it makes up a part of the lyrics that Lenardo has sung to Meister to complement Meister's abilities as a poet.

Composition: [1826].

Manuscript: Private hands.

First Publication: *Wilhelm Meister's Travels* in *German Romance* (1827), IV, 250.

Texts Consulted: *Wilhelm Meister's Travels* (1827); *Wilhelm Meister's Travels* (Rev. Ed., 1839); *Wilhelm Meister's Travels* (New Ed., 1842); *Wilhelm Meister's Travels* (People's Ed., 1874); *Sotheby's Catalogue* (MS facsimile, 1979), p. 267.

Copy-text: *Wilhelm Meister's Travels* (1842).

Textual Notes: The Sotheby manuscript was listed for sale on 14 March, 1979, Lot 312. This copy of the poem is signed "T. Carlyle."; and it is dated (by Sotheby's, but not on the manuscript facsimile) "Dumfries, 27 May 1865."

Variants:

1   now] round (1842)
8   On and on, my way] Now my weary way (1842)

9
[Dark Chain]

Commentary: This poem by Goethe was included in a packet of gifts sent to the Carlyles at their home in Comley Bank. The delight both felt upon receiving this packet from Germany is graphically expressed in a letter of 11 August, 1827, that Carlyle wrote to his mother:

> News came directly after breakfast that the packet from Goethe had arrived in Leith! . . . the daintiest *boxie* you ever saw! So carefully packed, so neatly and tastefully contrived was everything. There was a copy of Goethe's poems in 5 beautiful little volumes *"for the valued marriage-pair Carlyle"*; two other little books for myself; then two medals, one of Goethe himself, and another of his father and mother;

and lastly the prettiest wrought-iron necklace with a little figure of the poet's face set in gold "for my dear spouse," and a most dashing pocket-book for me. In the box containing the necklace, and in each pocket of the pocket-book were cards, each with a verse of poetry on it in the old masters [sic] hand; all these I will translate to you by and by, as well as the long letter which lay at the bottom of it all, one of the kindest and gravest epistles I have ever read. (*Letters,* IV, 244-245)

Carlyle's honorific letter to Goethe of 20 August is not any less enthusiastic:

. . . no Royal present could have gratified us more. These Books with their Inscriptions, these Autographs and tasteful ornaments, will be precious in other generations than ours. Of the Necklace in particular I am bound to mention that it is reposited among the most valued jewels, and set apart for "great occasions," as an *ernste Zierde* [translated by Carlyle, "so grave a tag"] fit only to be worn before Poets and intellectual Men. Accept our heartiest thanks for such friendly memorials of a relation . . . we must always regard among the most estimable of our life. (*Letters,* IV, 246-247)

Jane seems to have included a poem in thanks for the necklace, and added the following postcript to this letter: "My heartfelt thanks to the Poet for his graceful gift, which I prize more than a necklace of diamonds, and kiss with truest regard—" (*Letters,* IV, 249).

C. E. Norton in *The Correspondence Between Goethe and Carlyle* describes the necklace as being of "delicate wrought iron (such as German ladies, having given up then jewels, were in the habit of wearing after the battle of Jena) . . ." (p. 30).

Composition: [1827?].

Manuscript: Private hands.

First Publication: *Correspondence Between Goethe and Carlyle* (1887), p. 30.

Texts Consulted: MS; *Correspondence Between Goethe and Carlyle.*

Copy-text: MS.

Textual Notes: Carlyle's translation of Goethe's poem, which was on the third card that accompanied the necklace for Jane, is here given from the manuscript copy which is in the possession of the Carlyle descendants. The Norton version differs slightly from the transcribed copy in the editors' possession.

Variants:

1   mirror] mirror, (Norton)
1   smiling,] smiling
2   light] light,
3   wife] Wife
3   grace] grace,
4   wife] Wife
4   husband] Husband

10
The Osculation of the Stars

Commentary: In a letter of 12 November, 1830, to his brother John, Carlyle remarks that he has sent to *Fraser's Magazine* "(*Nimmo* and other trifles)" (*Letters*, V, 191).

Composition: [By February, 1831?].

Manuscript: Yale University.

First Publication: *Fraser's Magazine*, III, no. 13 (February, 1831), 16.

Texts Consulted: MS: *Fraser's Magazine*; Tennyson, "Poetry," p. 174.

Copy-text: *Fraser's Magazine*.

Textual Notes: The poem was given the title "The Kissing of the Stars" in the manuscript, and is followed by "(From the German)" on the same line. The title is underlined twice, and the manuscript is signed "T. C. *reddidit*[.]" In the absence of sufficient evidence, the date suggested for composition is the latest possible date. But, as Tennyson argues, it seems "almost certain" that it was sent along with "Nimmo" to *Fraser's Magazine* in 1830, which would suggest an earlier date ("Poetry," p. 174). Barrett is less certain and places the poem in the Craigenputtoch period (1828-1834).

Variants:

4   years,] years (MS)
6]   "fast" written above a cancelled "now" in the MS
7   love's] Love's

9   god-consecrate] God-consecrate
10   for ever] forever
11]   "was" (after "Late") cancelled in the MS
11]   "was" written above a cancelled "that" (after "it") in the MS
15   look,] look
16   she] She
16   kindly,] kindly
17   kiss] Kiss
17   took] took,
18]   "stern hap" written above a cancelled "our Fate" in the MS
19   god-consecrate] God-consecrate

11
[Mason-Lodge]

Commentary: This poem is the famous translation of Goethe's *Symbolum*. In a letter to John Sterling of 17 January, 1837, Carlyle copies the poem in German and then adds: "Is not that a piece of psalmody? It seems to me like a piece of marching music to the great brave Teutonic kindred as they march through the waste of time—that section of eternity they appointed for" (*Letters*, IX, 117). Carlyle's poem is one of the rare instances in which the translation actually is superior to the original, what Kuno Francke has called "a masterpiece of divinatory interpretation."[1]

Composition: [Late 1842 or early 1843?].

Manuscript: Yale University; Huntington Library MS 34594; State Library of Victoria, Melbourne.

First Publication: *Past and Present* (1843), p. 318.

Texts Consulted: MSS; *Past and Present* (1843; 2nd ed., 1845; People's Ed., 1872).

Copy-text: *Past and Present* (2nd ed., 1845).

Textual Notes: In the second edition of *Past and Present* (1845), the fourth stanza is added. The Huntington manuscript, no doubt written at a later date because of the shaky hand, lacks the first stanza, and at the end of the poem is added: "one last word: *Wir heissen euch hoffen*. We bid you be of hope. Adieu for this time." The Victoria manuscript lacks the first four stanzas, and is dated "16 May 1844[.]"

Variants:

6-7] The Future hides in it [caret, above n.l.] gladness [g under-
 lined twice] & sorrow; (HMS)

7 Gladness and sorrow] Good hap and sorrow (1843)

12 Stands [cancelled]] Veiled, (HMS)

15 silent!] silent. (HMS)

18 and error,] & error; ["error" cancelled and "error" then
 written above] (HMS)

20 misgiving.] misgiving (HMS)

21 Voices,–] voices (HMS)

22 Heard are] Voice of (1843)

23 Ages:] Ages; (1872)

24 'Choose well; your] 'Choose well, your (1843); "Choose
 (1872); "Choose well, y^r (HMS)

26 Here] "here (HMS)

27 stillness;] stillness, (HMS)

30 not.'] not." (1872)

Citation:

[1]"Carlyle, and Goethe's *Symbolum*," *Philological Quarterly*, 6
(April, 1927), 99.

12

The Nightingale

Commentary: This translation was written out just two weeks before
 Jane's sudden death on 21 April, 1866, and just five days after
 Carlyle's election as Lord Rector of Edinburgh University on 2
 April.

Manuscript: private hands.

Composition: 7 April, 1866.

First Publication: *Archiv für das Studium der Neureren Sprachen und
 Literaturen*, 164 (1933), 252-253.

Texts Consulted: MS; *Archiv*.

Copy-texts: MS.

Textual Notes: The verse was sent to Carlyle by Goethe on 9 May,
 1828, but was not translated until 1866. Following the poem
 at the left is the signature: "For the 9th of next May / 1828";
 at the right: "(signed) Goethe."; at the bottom: "[Translated by
 T. Carlyle (7 April 1866)] [.]"

Emendation:
    4   again] ag^n (MS)

Notes to the Poems of Jane Welsh Carlyle

1
The Rival Brothers

Commentary: This fragment in Jane's hand is dated 1824, and is only
part of a five-act tragedy — now lost — written by her in 1815
when she was fourteen. The play was sent to C. H. Terrot, later
Bishop of Edinburgh, who appreciated the "considerable inven-
tion," found the "language . . . uniformly correct," although the
"metre sometimes deficient." To this evaluation Terrot added,
it is "much beyond what I expected to find it" (*Love Letters*, p.
168n.). Carlyle also seems to have read the original, complete
version, and in a letter of 18 February, 1823, he reports that
he had read it "with more real enjoyment than any regular tragedy
has given me of late. I am not going to flatter you about the
promises of genius which it affords, tho' I must say that for a
girl of fourteen, it seems a very curious affair" (*Letters*, II, 291).

Composition: [1815].

Manuscript: National Library of Scotland MS Acc. 4463.

First Publication: *Letters*, (1977), VII, 361-368.

Texts Consulted: MS; *Letters*.

Copy-text: MS.

Textual Notes: In anticipation of authorial intention, punctuation has
been added, where necessary, to the speakers' names. All other
punctuation alterations have been listed under *Emendations*.

Emendations:

11]   friend's] friends
19]   I've] Ive
32-33]   written in the right hand margin of the MS.
35]   unforeseen] unforseen
41]   father's] fathers
47]   ne'er] neer
44]   which] w^h
51]   left.] left
61]   father's] fathers
5]   would] w^d
6]   which] w^h
10]   side.] side
12]   would] w^d
21]   which your . . . your] w^h y^r . . . y^r

30]   father's] fathers
40]   which] w^h
41]   thee] the
48]   would] w^d
55]   after "comes;" is written and cancelled "he must not see
       you"[.]"
56]   here.] here
63]   would] w^d
63]   parents'] parents
64]   mistake.] mistake
75]   tyrant's] tyrants
79]   and] &
85]   I'll] Ill
86]   woman's] womans
99]   hope.] hope
6]   "oerspread" is cancelled and "oerpowered" is written above.
6]   o'erpowered] oerpowered]
18]   thee] the
33]   Adelaide's] Adelaides
34]   Abelaide's] Adelaides
38]   "glorious" is cancelled and "joyous" is written above.
42]   and] &
45]   which] w^h
46]   and] &
56]   Angel's] Angels

2
[My Loved Minstrel]

Commentary: The poem may well have been composed in response
to Byron's removal from England in April of 1816, and is note-
worthy as documentation of Jane's early and continued disciple-
ship, a discipleship which was later encouraged and fostered by
her suitor Carlyle during his own period of identification so graph-
ically written about in *Sartor Resartus.* Carlyle was finally able
to put Byron behind him, to close the door of romantic despair;
Jane, on the other hand, maintained her kinship well beyond her
formative years and, in fact, employs a type of Byronic wit in

her own poems.   Unlike Carlyle's, her bridge to *Manfred* never actually collapsed.

Composition: [After April, 1816].

Manuscript: Edinburgh University Library.

First Publication: Ian M. Campbell, ed. *Thomas and Jane: selected letters from the Edinburgh University Library* (Edinburgh: Privately printed, 1980), p. [viii].

Texts Consulted: MS; Campbell.

Copy-text: MS.

Textual Notes: The manuscript is signed "Jane Baillie Welsh" and is dated "1816[.]" The original date was 1817, but the 7 is written over, apparently in Carlyle's hand. The date is underlined and in the right margin lines 13-15 are blocked, also an editorial characteristic of Carlyle's.

3
[I Love the Mountain Torrent]

Commentary: In a letter to Jane of 17? June, 1822, Carlyle calls the poem, among others sent, "the best of all" (*Letters,* II, 132).

Composition: [June, 1822].

Manuscript: National Library of Scotland MS 2884.14.

First Publication: *Love Letters* (1909), II, 344-345.

Texts Consulted: MS; *Love Letters*.

Copy-text: MS.

Textual Notes: The poem is published here for the first time in complete form. In the *Love Letters,* Alexander Carlyle deletes the last four lines and alters the stanzaic presentation.

Variants:

1	dashing,] dashing (*Love Letters*)
2	Downward,] Downward
2	hoarse,] hoarse;
3	fury,] fury
4	course—] course.
5	thunder,] thunder
6	skies,] skies;
7	clouds,] clouds

8　　　death-ful] deathful
8　　　destroys—] destroys.
12　　broking] brooking
12　　control—] control.

4

The Wish

Commentary: Jane composed this poem in response to Carlyle's of the
　　　same title; see the note under Carlyle entry no. 3.
Composition: [1822].
Manuscript: National Library of Scotland MS 2884.15.
First Publication: *Love Letters* (1909), II, 343-44.
Texts Consulted. MS; *Love Letters*.
Copy-text: MS.
Textual Notes: Alexander Carlyle's version of the poem in the *Love
　　　Letters* is significantly different from the manuscript. It is re-
　　　motely possible that he was using a different manuscript, but
　　　more likely this is another example of his editorial indiscretion.
　　　In a manuscript, there are three exclamation points after the title,
　　　and after lines 4, 8 24 and 28. Also, in the right margin after
　　　line 20 is written: ("Oh lord." Finally, the whole of the last
　　　stanza is absent from Alexander's edition.
Variants.
　　　4　　　young] young (*Love Letters*)
　　　4　　　fresh] fresh
　　　6　　　sound] sound
　　　7　　　hate,] hate
　　　9　　　wile;] wile
　　　11　　Making] Leaving
　　　12　　turn'd—] turned
　　　13　　nature] one might
　　　13　　sees] see
　　　13　　tears,] tears
　　　14　　dewy] sparkling
　　　14　　drops,] drops
　　　14　　shed;] shed,

15   Mother's] mother's
16   head—] head.
17   nature] one might
17   hears] hear
18   breathes;] breathes
19   flies,] flies
20   leaves—] leaves.
21   days,] days
22   *one*] One
22   lot] fate
22   share;] share—
23   soul depths] soul-depths
23   gaze,] gaze
24   see] find
25   one] One
26   own;] own.

5
Lines to Lord Byron
From his daughter, Ada

Commentary: In a letter to Carlyle of [1 July, 1822], Jane suggests
that the subject of this poem would be suitable for Carlyle: "Will
you try it? And address to Lord Byron from his daughter. If she
is *a genius* she might be writing verses by this time—those people
are always in my head—I began to think yesterday, in church, of
his child's feelings towards him . . . (*Letters*, II, 144). In a letter
of [11 July, 1822] she briefly adds: "I hope you have made some-
thing of Ada—I have made a precious nursery song of it" (*Let-
ters*, II, 147). In response to Jane, Carlyle writes on 13 July:
"I did my best endeavour to conceive the feelings of poor Ada,
and throw some ornament over them . . . and I *intended* to draw
a very notable moral over the whole . . ." (*Letters*, II, 147-148).
Carlyle apparently never came back to the subject.
Composition: [June, 1822].
Manuscript: Untraced.
First Publication: *Love Letters* (1909), II, 348-349.
Texts Consulted: *Love Letters*.

Copy-text: *Love Letters*.

Textual Notes: Evidenced by his liberal alteration of other poems, it is likely that Alexander Carlyle has here once again changed the stanzaic presentation, although of course this cannot be established in the absence of a manuscript or other text.

6

Verses Written at Midnight

Commentary: Referring to this poem and to Jane's general abilities as a poet, Carlyle writes to her on 13 July, 1822: "Those verses you have sent me are proofs at once of your genius and diligence. You can already versify with great ease and correctness. . . . The lines 'written at midnight' have something in them which is to me exceedingly beautiful and pathetic: I have read them over often; and found much to admire and not one expression to blame" (*Letters*, II, 149).

Composition: [June-July? 1822].

Manuscript: Untraced.

First Publication: *Love Letters* (1909), II, 349-350.

Texts Consulted: *Love Letters*.

Copy-text: *Love Letters*.

Textual Notes: See the note under entry no. 5.

7

Lines On — I Don't Know What

Commentary: From the subject matter and style, it seems likely that this is one of "those verses" sent along to Carlyle with "Verses Written at Midnight."

Composition: [1822?].

Manuscript: National Library of Scotland, MS 2884.13.

First Publication: Unpublished.

Texts Consulted: MS.

Copy-text: MS.

Textual Notes. In line 6, "That" in the original is struck and "That" then written in the margin beside it; at the end of line 9, "again" is indented on a second line; and, in line 29; "[crisons]" is an interpolated reading.

8
[The Setting Sun]

Commentary: Like "Lines on—I Don't Know What," this poem seems written from Jane's especial romantic spirit of 1822, and curiously enough appears Blakean in its personification of nature's spirit.
Composition: [1822?].
Manuscript: National Library of Scotland, MS 2884.16.
First Publication: Unpublished.
Texts Consulted: MS.
Copy-text: MS.
Textual Notes: In lines 21 and 22 appear the names Menischeh and Afrasiab, both of which are interpolated readings because of Jane's obscure handwriting.
Variants:

1]   "sun" is cancelled, and above it is written "sun."
24]   "sun" is cancelled, and after it is written "sun."

9
[With Song and Dance Grotesque]

Commentary: This darkly satiric poem seems out of mood for Jane in the early 1820s. Yet the uncommon use of the word *orisons* in line 7 parallels that of the 1822 "Lines On—I Don't Know What."
Composition: [1822?].
Manuscript: National Library of Scotland, MS, 546.49.
First Publication: Unpublished.
Texts Consulted; MS.
Copy-text: MS.
Textual Notes: In manuscript, each stanza is separated by a short rule, and at the bottom is the signature "J Welsh[.]"

10
[Dark Chain]

Commentary: This poem seems written in response to the gift of a necklace and poem sent by Goethe; see Carlyle's translation of the poem, under entry no. 9.

Composition: [1827?].
Manuscript: Private hands.
Publication: Unpublished.
Texts Consulted: MS.
Copy-text: MS.

11
[Nay, This Is Hope]

Commentary: This poem is written in response to Carlyle's "Cui
    Bono"; see under Carlyle, entry no. 13. If true, then Jane seems
    to be responding to the published version of Carlyle's poem, for
    Froude claims that Jane's poem is dated "1830" in "one of Mrs.
    Carlyle's note-books" (Froude, II, 421).
Composition: [1830?].
Manuscript: Untraced.
First Publication: Froude (1882), II, 421.
Texts Consulted: Froude.
Copy-text: Froude.

Notes to the Translations of Jane Welsh Carlyle

1
The Fisher

Commentary: Jane complained on several occasions about the difficulties she was having with the translation, about how embarrassed she was by it, and about how relieved she was to be rid of her "unfortunate fisher" *Letters,* I, 375-376; II, 114, 130). Carlyle's comments, together with his version and notes on it, were sent by return mail, no doubt in a letter of 27 May, 1822:

> "The Fisher [underlined twice] is a very happy and ingenious translation; tolerable in all, considering the shackles you had to move in. I will not point out the weak parts of it; you see them clearly enough yourself, as I observe. It is more difficult to point out a remedy; scarce possible perhaps, without a further departure from the letter of the original. Some alterations I have attempted with poor success. The chief ones are founded on a slight misconception, you seem to have fallen into, with regard to the *scene* of the poem, which I apprehend is not a river but the Sea; our hero not being an *Amateur* Angler but a vulgar hard-working Fisherman, plying his craft in a dingy *Coble,* afloat upon some fair bay (that of Naples, for example), where the beauty of the deep & the influence of the climate conspire to produce in the Mind a certain indescribable longing for the ocean, a kind of affection for it, which (Mad. de Stael thinks—see her Corrinne — & Germany) Goethe has very ably represented & shadowed forth in this small tragedy." (*Letters,* II, 120)

See also notes under Carlyle's translation, entry no. 1.

Composition: [May, 1822].

Manuscript: Nationl Library of Scotland, MS 529.21.

First Publication: *Love Letters* (1909), II, 342-343.

Texts Consulted: MS; *Love Letters*; *Letters,* II, 121-122.

Copy-text: MS.

Textual Notes: Carlyle gives it the title, "The Fisher by Jane," and underlines it twice except "by" which is underlined once. In the *Love Letters,* Alexander Carlyle prints a combination of Jane's translation and Carlyle's correction (see under Carlyle's translation, entry no. 1). Only stanzas 3, 5, 7, in Alexander's text, are taken from Jane's version. The manuscript is in Carlyle's hand.

Emendation:
    11   and] &

Variants:
    10   Ah] Ah! (*Love Letters*)
    11   man] man,
    13   "Doth] Does
    13   Moon] moon
    15   become] return
    28   love's] Love's

2
An Indian Mother's Lament

Commentary: The poem seems to have been translated during May of 1822, while Jane was reading Chateaubriand's *Atala, ou les amours de deux sauvates dans le desert* (Paris, 1801). Carlyle apparently had sent a copy of *Atala* to her, and in a letter of 29th [25th? May, 1822], she responds, "I do not like Atala— What tempted you to send me such nonsense? (*Letters*, II, 114). In a letter of 27 May, 1822, Carlyle appeals to Jane to send by return what "trash" verses she has, and "those from Atala; it is of the kind I like" (*Letters*, II, 117).
Composition: [May? 1822].
Manuscript: Untraced.
First Publication: *Love Letters* (1909), II, 343.
Texts Consulted: *Love Letters*.
Copy-text: *Love Letters*.

3
A Love Song

Commentary: In a letter to Jane of 17? June, 1822, Carlyle praises the success of this translation, but says that the subject of the "hesitating lover" does not interest him (*Letters*, II, 132). Alexander Carlyle indicates that it is "Translated from the Provençal" (*Love Letters*, II, 346).

Composition: [June, 1822].
Manuscript: Untraced.
First Publication: *Love Letters* (1909), II, 346.
Texts Consulted: *Love Letters*.
Copy-text: *Love Letters*.

4
[From East to West]

Commentary: In a letter to Jane of 17? June, 1822, Carlyle says of
this poem, "the little epigram from the Provençal Satyrist is also
a favourite with me; it seems rendered with great spirit and live-
liness" (*Letters*, II, 132).
Composition: [1822].
Manuscript: National Library of Scotland MS 2884.17.
First Publication: *Love Letters* (1909), II, 345.
Text Consulted: MS; *Love Letters*.
Copy-text: MS.
Textual Notes: Alexander Carlyle gives the poem the title, "A 'Sir-
vente,'" and points out that it is "Translated from Pierre Car-
denal," a thirteenth-century French satirist and wit (*Love Letters*,
II, 345). In his text, Alexander deletes line 9, and reverses the
order of lines 13-14.
Variants:

1	told,] told (*Love Letters*)
3	agree,] agree
4	me;] me.
7	fools,] fools
8	give—] give.
10	half] one-half
10	done;] done
11	heard,] heard
12	calling-card—] calling card.
13	enough,] enough;
14	who] that
14	worth;] worth
15	treat,] treat
16	'come,] "come
16	folks,] folks
16	eat!'] eat"!

Index

The poems followed by (A) indicate autograph poems and questionable attributions; by (T) translations; and by (J) for Jane's work. The number following the entry is the number given to each poem, respectively.